BioCritiques

Bloom's BioCritiques

STEPHEN CRANE

Edited and with an introduction by
Harold Bloom
Sterling Professor of the Humanities
Yale University

CHELSEA HOUSE PUBLISHERS
Philadelphia

10 9 8 7 6 5 4 3 2 1

Library of Congress Cataloging-in-Publication Data

Stephen Crane / Harold Bloom, ed.
        p. cm. -- (Bloom's Biocritiques)
Includes bibliographical references and index.
  ISBN 0-7910-6375-5
  1. Crane, Stephen, 1871-1900--Criticism and interpretation. I.
Bloom,
Harold. II. Series.
  PS1449.C85 Z925 2002
  813'.4--dc21
                                        2002005627

Chelsea House Publishers
1974 Sproul Road, Suite 400
Broomall, PA 19008-0914

http://www.chelseahouse.com

Contributing editor: Robert Gunn

Layout by EJB Publishing Services

CONTENTS

User's Guide

These volumes are designed to introduce the reader to the life and work of the world's literary masters. Each volume begins with Harold Bloom's essay "The Work in the Writer" and a volume-specific introduction also written by Professor Bloom. Following these unique introductions is an engaging biography that discusses the major life events and important literary accomplishments of the author under consideration.

Furthermore, each volume includes an original critique that not only traces the themes, symbols, and ideas apparent in the author's works, but strives to put those works into cultural and historical perspectives. In addition to the original critique is a brief selection of significant critical essays previously published on the author and his or her works followed by a concise and informative chronology of the writer's life. Finally, each volume concludes with a bibliography of the writer's works, a list of additional readings, and an index of important themes and ideas.

HAROLD BLOOM

The Work in the Writer

Literary biography found its masterpiece in James Boswell's *Life of Samuel Johnson*. Boswell, when he treated Johnson's writings, implicitly commented upon Johnson as found in his work, even as in the great critic's life. Modern instances of literary biography, such as Richard Ellmann's lives of W. B. Yeats, James Joyce, and Oscar Wilde, essentially follow in Boswell's pattern.

That the writer somehow is in the work, we need not doubt, though with William Shakespeare, writer-of-writers, we almost always need to rely upon pure surmise. The exquisite rancidities of the Problem Plays or Dark Comedies seem to express an extraordinary estrangement of Shakespeare from himself. When we read or attend *Troilus and Cressida* and *Measure for Measure*, we may be startled by particular speeches of Ulysses in the first play, or of Vincentio in the second. These speeches, of Ulysses upon hierarchy or upon time, or of Duke Vincentio upon death, are too strong either for their contexts or for the characters of their speakers. The same phenomenon occurs with Parolles, the military impostor of *All's Well That Ends Well*. Utterly disgraced, he nevertheless affirms: "Simply the thing I am/Shall make me live."

In Shakespeare, more even than in his peers, Dante and Cervantes, meaning always starts itself again through excess or overflow. The strongest of Shakespeare's creatures—Falstaff, Hamlet, Iago, Lear, Cleopatra—have an exuberance that is fiercer than their plays can contain. If Ben Jonson was at all correct in his complaint that "Shakespeare wanted art," it could have been only in a sense that he may not have intended. Where do the personalities of Falstaff or Hamlet touch a limit? What was it in Shakespeare that made the two parts of *Henry IV* and *Hamlet* into "plays unlimited"? Neither Falstaff nor Hamlet will be stopped: their wit, their beautiful, laughing speech, their intensity of being—all these are virtually infinite.

In what ways do Falstaff and Hamlet manifest the writer in the work? Evidently, we can never know, or know enough to answer with any authority. But what would happen if we reversed the question, and asked: How did the work form the writer, Shakespeare?

Of Shakespeare's inwardness, his biography tells us nothing. And yet, to an astonishing extent, Shakespeare created our inwardness. At the least, we can speculate that Shakespeare so lived his life as to conceal the depths of his nature, particularly as he rather prematurely aged. We do not have Shakespeare on Shakespeare, as any good reader of the Sonnets comes to realize: they do not constitute a key that unlocks his heart. No sequence of sonnets could be less confessional or more powerfully detached from the poet's self.

The German poet and universal genius, Goethe, affords a superb contrast to Shakespeare. Of Goethe's life, we know more than everything; I wonder sometimes if we know as much about Napoleon or Freud or any other human being who ever has lived, as we know about Goethe. Everywhere, we can find Goethe in his work, so much so that Goethe seems to crowd the writing out, just as Byron and Oscar Wilde seem to usurp their own literary accomplishments. Goethe, cunning beyond measure, nevertheless invested a rival exuberance in his greatest works that could match his personal charisma. The sublime outrageousness of the Second Part of *Faust*, or of the greater lyric and meditative poems, form a Counter-Sublime to Goethe's own daemonic intensity.

Goethe was fascinated by the daemonic in himself; we can doubt that Shakespeare had any such interests. Evidently, Shakespeare abandoned his acting career just before he composed *Measure for Measure* and *Othello*. I surmise that the egregious interventions by Vincentio and Iago displace the actor's energies into a new kind of mischief-making, a fresh opening to a subtler playwriting-within-the-play.

But what had opened Shakespeare to this new awareness? The answer is the work in the writer, *Hamlet* in Shakespeare. One can go further: it was not so much the play, *Hamlet*, as the character Hamlet, who changed Shakespeare's art forever.

Hamlet's personality is so large and varied that it rivals Goethe's own. Ironically Goethe's Faust, his Hamlet, has no personality at all, and is as colorless as Shakespeare himself seems to have chosen to be. Yet nothing could be more colorful than the Second Part of *Faust*, which is peopled by an astonishing array of monsters, grotesque devils, and classical ghosts.

A contrast between Shakespeare and Goethe demonstrates that in each—but in very different ways—we can better find the work in the person, than we can discover that banal entity, the person in the work. Goethe to many of his contemporaries, seemed to be a mortal god. Shakespeare, so far as we know, seemed an affable, rather ordinary fellow, who aged early and became somewhat withdrawn. Yet Faust, though Mephistopheles battles for his soul, is hardly worth the trouble unless you take him as an idea and not as a person. Hamlet is nearly every-idea-in-one, but he is precisely a personality and a person.

Would Hamlet be so astonishingly persuasive if his father's ghost did not haunt him? Falstaff is more alive than Prince Hal, who says that the devil haunts him in the shape of an old fat man. Three years before composing the final *Hamlet*, Shakespeare invented Falstaff, who then never ceased to haunt his creator. Falstaff and Hamlet may be said to best represent the work in the writer, because their influence upon Shakespeare was prodigious. W.H. Auden accurately observed that Falstaff possesses infinite energy: never tired, never bored, and absolutely both witty and happy until Hal's rejection destroys him. Hamlet too has infinite energy, but in him it is more curse than blessing.

Falstaff and Hamlet can be said to occupy the roles in Shakespeare's invented world that Sancho Panza and Don Quixote possess in Cervantes's. Shakespeare's plays from 1610 on (starting with *Twelfth Night*) are thus analogous to the Second Part of Cervantes's epic novel. Sancho and the Don overtly jostle Cervantes for authorship in the Second Part, even as Cervantes battles against the impostor who has pirated a continuation of his work. As a dramatist, Shakespeare manifests the work in the writer more indirectly. Falstaff's prose genius is revived in the scapegoating of Malvolio by Maria and Sir Toby Belch, while Falstaff's darker insights are developed by Feste's melancholic wit. Hamlet's intellectual resourcefulness, already deadly, becomes poisonous in Iago and in Edmund. Yet we have not crossed into the deeper abysses of the work in the writer in later Shakespeare.

No fictive character, before or since, is Falstaff's equal in self-trust. Sir John, whose delight in himself is contagious, has total confidence both in his self-awareness and in the resources of his language. Hamlet, whose self is as strong, and whose language is as copious, nevertheless distrusts both the self and language. Later Shakespeare is, as it were, much under the influence both of Falstaff and of Hamlet, but they tug him in opposite directions. Shakespeare's own copiousness of language is well-nigh incredible: a vocabulary in excess of twenty-one thousand words, almost eighteen hundred of which he coined himself. And of his word-hoard, nearly half are used only once each, as though the perfect setting for each had been found, and need not be repeated. Love for language and faith in language are Falstaffian attributes. Hamlet will darken both that love and that faith in Shakespeare, and perhaps the Sonnets can best be read as Falstaff and Hamlet counterpointing against one another.

Can we surmise how aware Shakespeare was of Falstaff and Hamlet, once they had played themselves into existence? *Henry IV, Part I* appeared in six quarto editions during Shakespeare's lifetime; *Hamlet* possibly had four. Falstaff and Hamlet were played again and again at the Globe, but Shakespeare knew also that they were being read, and he must have had contact with some of those readers. What would it have been like to discuss Falstaff or Hamlet with one of their early readers (presumably also part of their audience at the Globe), if you were the creator of such demiurges? The question would seem nonsensical to most Shakespeare scholars, but then these days they tend to be either ideologues or moldy figs. How can we recover the uncanniness of Falstaff and of Hamlet, when they now have become so familiar?

A writer's influence upon himself is an unexplored problem in criticism, but such an influence is never free from anxieties. The biocritical problem (which this series attempts to explore) can be divided into two areas, difficult to disengage fully. Accomplished works affect the author's life, and also affect her subsequent writings. It is simpler for me to surmise the effect of *Mrs. Dalloway* and *To the Lighthouse* upon Woolf's late *Between the Acts*, than it is to relate Clarissa Dalloway's suicide and Lily Briscoe's capable endurance in art to the tragic death and complex life of Virginia Woolf.

There are writers whose lives were so vivid that they seem sometimes to obscure the literary achievement: Byron, Wilde, Malraux, Hemingway. But most major Western writers do not live that exuberantly, and the greatest of all, Shakespeare, sometimes appears to have adopted the personal mask of colorlessness. And yet there are heroes of literature who struggled titanically with their own eras—Tolstoy, Milton, Victor Hugo—who nevertheless matter more for their works than their lives.

There are great figures—Emily Dickinson, Wallace Stevens, Willa Cather—who seem to have had so little of the full intensity of life when compared to the vitality of their work, that we might almost speak of the work in the work, rather than even of the work in a person. Emily Brontë might well be the extreme instance of such a visionary, surpassing William Blake in that one regard.

I conclude this general introduction to a series of literary bio-critiques by stating a tentative formula or principle for gauging the many ways in which the work influences the person and her subsequent, later work. Our influence upon ourselves is always related to the Shakespearean invention of self-overhearing, which I have written about in several other contexts. Life, as well as poetry and prose, is overheard rather than simply heard. The writer listens to herself as though she were somebody else, and the will to change begins to operate. The forces that live in us include the prior work we have done, and the dreams and waking visions that evade our dismissals.

Introduction

The effect of Stephen Crane's best writings upon his short but turbulent life was immense and fortunate, but tuberculosis killed him at twenty-eight, and what his future literary development might have been remains problematic. His life, like his work, has been a paradigm for major American authors, Ernest Hemingway in particular.

Stephen Crane's aesthetic achievement is slender in bulk, surprisingly so despite his early death. *The Red Badge of Courage* is a permanent short novel. Three stories—"The Open Boat," "The Blue Hotel," and "The Bride Comes to Yellow Sky"—and four of five brief lyrics are also of authentic aesthetic merit. The rest of his work, starting with the novel, *Maggie: A Girl of the Streets*, is undistinguished. Yet Crane's promise was extraordinary, and earned him the friendship of two great novelists, Joseph Conrad and Henry James, who were fascinated by Crane's natural mastery of literary impressionism.

Crane was the youngest of fourteen children of a Methodist minister, and lost his mother when he was twenty. Some five years later he began a deep involvement with Cora Taylor, the madam of a bordello in Florida. Her notoriety prompted the couple to settle in England, where they lived until Crane died in a German sanitarium.

The aesthetic gap between *The Red Badge of Courage*, and Crane's handful of outstanding stories and poems—on the one side—and the rest of his work is disconcerting. Aside from *Maggie*, which is just about readable, Crane's other novels are forgotten: *George's Mother*, *The Third Violet*, *Active Service*, and the unfinished *The O'Ruddy*. The miracle of *The Red Badge of Courage* was not repeated, good as the three best stories and three or four lyrics have proved to be. What was it about the influence upon Crane of his own masterpiece that wasted his genius?

The poet John Berryman, in his critical biography of Crane, rather impressively reduces his subject's erotic life to a classic Freudian plot that is over-determined: the Rescue Fantasy. The ideal female object of desire should be an older, fallen woman: a clear displacement of the mother. Whenever Crane incorporated the Rescue Fantasy in his writing, he produced pathos. Fortunately, *The Red Badge of Courage*, though amazingly persuasive, is a war fantasy, fairly free of Crane's erotic obsession. When he wrote *Red Badge*, Crane had never seen a battle. As a war correspondent, he later observed fighting in Cuba and in Greece, but his account of the Battle of Chancellorsville is a pure act of the impressionistic imagination.

Crane's subject in *Red Badge*, as all his critics agree, is fear. That fear *may* have an origin in Crane's rebellion against the Evangelical Methodism of his family, or again it may be the fear of incest, expressed as the shame of being afraid in battle. Critics have noted also the Biblical touch in Crane's vision of battle. Henry Fleming, Crane's surrogate in *Red Badge*, transcends his fear through anger, a curiously prophetic kind of anger, marked by irony and by transference of hatred from the familial context, and from self, to the enemy. When the book concludes, Henry is a war hero, exemplary for the clear-sightedness that he can maintain even in the tumult and confusions of battle.

Something in Stephen Crane experienced a resurrection from fear in Henry Fleming. The apotheosis of Henry is not Tolstoyan: he is not reborn through a selfless love of his fellow soldiers. The peculiar power of *Red Badge* is in the sublime isolation of the hero's triumph over fear. Tolstoy, even in *Hadji Murad*, which celebrates its Chechen epic hero, is most himself when he describes men in groups, suffering both a communal anguish and a communal ecstasy. Stephen Crane, as befits an American imagination, sees and relates an individual struggle within a larger destiny.

For Crane, there truly was one story only that he had to tell: that of his own emergence from family romance and its sorrows. He tells the story supremely well in *The Red Badge of Courage*, but then never again could he compose a full-scale saga. He is not the only American with a solitary masterpiece, and he can be said to have prophesied a dilemma that is with us still.

NORMA JEAN LUTZ

Biography of Stephen Crane

An Open Boat

On the afternoon of December 31st, 1896, stevedores loaded cargo into the hold of the *Commodore*, a coal-burning tug docked at the port of Jacksonville, Florida and bound for Cuba. The cargo of firearms and ammunition would be used to aid the insurgents looking to overthrow the Spanish hold on the island. Due to the Cuban uprising, the town's population had swelled almost overnight, as Jacksonville had become a headquarters for Cuban leaders and operatives, gutsy newspaper reporters, and mercenaries. On assignment in Jacksonville, as a correspondent for the Bacheller-Johnson News Syndicate, was Stephen Crane, waiting to book passage on the first available vessel bound for the island. The uprising had brought on an increased US Navy presence at sea that made it difficult to gain passage to the island without being intercepted and turned back. When the *Commodore* pushed off and headed down the St. Johns River, Crane was aboard. Yet before the tug reached the open sea, it ran aground on a sand bar less than two miles from Jacksonville, where passengers and crew were obliged to remain until morning. When the *Commodore* was towed off the bar, no one examined the hull for possible damage. At sea, whitecaps tossed the boat violently, leaving many of the Cuban crewmembers seasick. Crane suffered no such agonies. Sleepless and unaffected, he made his way to the pilothouse, where he and Edward Murphy, the ship's captain, smoked cigars and traded stories late into the night. Although Crane had never been at sea before, Captain Murphy said he "behaved like a born sailor." [Stallman, 247]

Just as Crane settled into a corner of the pilothouse to sleep, the chief engineer burst in from below decks, shouting that the boiler room was flooding and the bilge pumps had failed. Crane followed the chief engineer and Captain Murphy to the engine room, which appeared to Crane to have been taken "from the middle kitchen of Hades":

> In the first place, it was insufferably warm, and the lights burned faintly in a way to cause mystic and gruesome shadows. There was a quantity of soap[y] seawater swirling and sweeping and swishing among machinery that roared and banged and clattered and steamed, and, in the second place, it was a devil of a ways down below. [Stallman, 246]

The crew formed a bucket brigade to keep water from reaching the boilers, and Crane helped, but the sea was gushing in from the hull faster than they could bail it out. The captain ordered a hotter fire, built of wood, oil, and alcohol, hoping to gain enough steam to reach a nearby island. When that failed, the captain ordered the lowering of the lifeboats.

The first boat, loaded with twelve Cubans and their baggage, pushed off safely. The second boat became caught on one of the davits. With several crewmembers, Crane struggled with the ropes, but no one could free the boat from the snarled turnbuckle. The boat weighed "as much as a Broadway cable-car," Crane said; "We could have pushed a little brick schoolhouse along a corduroy road as easily. . . ." [Stallman, 248] When by some means the boat finally was launched, it was overcrowded, as was the third. The last boat to be let over the side was an English dinghy, with barely enough room for two grown men. It contained four: Captain Murphy, Crane, the ship's cook, and a young oiler.

Out on the ocean, waves threatened to capsize the small boat, even as they continually bailed water; regardless, the captain ordered that they remain near the tug until it sank. As they crested a wave, they heard a cry; the third lifeboat was returning to the tug. There are varying accounts of why it did so: one was that the first mate had forgotten something, another that its occupants had encountered problems with the lifeboat itself. Whatever the reason, the sinking ship was shattered by pounding waves while the lifeboat's occupants were again aboard. Captain Murphy ordered his own group to make rafts of what remained of the boat. Three of the men leapt from the ship onto the makeshift rafts, while a fourth man dove into the dark, choppy water to his death.

For a time, the dinghy tried to tow the rafts, but this was an "absolute impossibility" as the gunwale of their boat dipped to "within six inches of the water's edge." In the New York *World*, Captain Murphy recounted, "There was an enormous sea running . . . [and] the waves were tremendous, as high as I have ever seen them hereabouts. They rolled in on us, threatening to dash us against the sinking tug, and we expected [at] every moment to be overthrown." [Stallman, 251] After the tug went down, the men who had struggled to remain near the rafts gave in to the wind and allowed themselves to be carried away. Crane manned one oar of the dinghy; the oiler, Billy Higgins, manned the other, and the ship's cook, Charles Montgomery, steered. The changing of positions in the tiny vessel required extreme caution, and the memory of the danger of it would haunt Crane throughout his life. The captain, his arm broken earlier by a lowering boat, sat pensive at the stern. Then Crane and another man alternately rowed and bailed, watching for a lighthouse or the dark mass on the horizon that meant land. Changing places in the boat was precarious at best and had to be done with extreme caution. The strenuous rowing kept the men warm, but as soon as they stopped their teeth chattered from the abrasive headwinds.

While one of the large lifeboats reached the shore by noon on Saturday, January 2, the dinghy continued its struggle at sea for another thirty hours—through the night, and in the noted presence of sharks—for by the time they could see land the waves were so steep that the captain ordered them to remain out of the breakers until morning. By seven o'clock on January 3, they braved the surf and made their way toward shore. There were only two lifebelts aboard the dinghy, and the Captain gave one to Crane and the other to the ship's steward. The next wave took them under, and the boat was smashed on the rocks. For nearly an hour, swimming toward shore, the men fought the unrelenting waves. The ship's cook was swept and dragged safely onto the beach first—onlookers had gathered slowly on the shore—as Captain Murphy held onto the keel of the overturned boat with his one functioning hand. Crane tried to assist Billy Higgins, who had been injured by flying debris and who had worked valiantly throughout the ordeal to row and steer the dinghy, but eventually he had to save himself. He had to jettison both his clothing and a chamois-skin money belt containing $700 in Spanish gold given to him by the news syndicate.

On shore, John Kitchell, a resident of Daytona, saw the men in the surf and realized that they were in desperate need of help. Throwing off his clothing, he dove into the water to assist them. Once Crane had been dragged ashore to safety, he saw the lifeless body of Higgins lying in the sand. Within minutes, as he recalled, people swarmed onto the beach bringing, the survivors hot coffee and blankets. While Murphy and Montgomery were taken to a nearby home, Crane spent the night at the home of Mr. and Mrs.

Lawrence Thompson near the Halifax River—a gesture in thanks for which Crane would later send to them a signed copy of *The Red Badge of Courage*.

In one of Crane's early pieces, "The Wreck of the *New Era*," he chronicled the shipwreck of the *New Era* of Bath, Maine, which ran aground in a dense fog off the New Jersey coast. The essay presages the sinking of the *Commodore*. It can be said that daring events of this kind would prove the impetus behind much of his writing, in particular the short story "The Open Boat". Crane was able to extract from harrowing events an aesthetic view that he translated into the "dirty realism" that characterizes much of his later fiction.

His Own Story

Stephen Crane was known to take pride in the fact that many of the relatives on his father's side were instrumental in settling and defending the English territory that would become the United States, specifically the state of New Jersey. Initially, the town of Montclair was known as Cranetown, after Jasper and Azariah Crane. He once said of his lineage, "I am about as much of a Jersey-man as you can find." [Stallman, 1]

The first member of the Crane family to arrive in the Colonies, the first Stephen Crane, came in late 17th century from England, possibly Wales. His grandson and namesake Stephen was a staunch patriot and led the Colonial Assemblies in New England. During the life of this second Stephen, two of his sons attained high rank in the military: one was a major general in the regular army, and the other Commodore of the Navy, while his third and youngest son served in the Essex Militia. This son, as Crane told the story, met his death at the hands of Hessian soldiers for refusing to divulge the location of a nearby American outpost. The middle son, the Commodore, was imprisoned on a British ship in the New York harbor. According to Crane, the military exploits of his father's side of the family during the Revolutionary War were historic: "[T]he Cranes were pretty hot people. . . ." [Stallman, 2]

Further down his father's family tree, Crane had relatives that served in the War of 1812, in a skirmish against Barbary pirates in 1815, and in notable conflicts during the Mexican-American War, and the American Civil War. From a young age Crane was dazzled by his father's ancestry, filled with larger-than-life characters. He wrote, "The man whose forefathers were men of courage, sympathy and wisdom . . . will stand the strain . . . like [a] thoroughbred horse [whose] nerves may be high, but in crisis he becomes the most reliable and enduring of men." [Sufrin, 10] As this self-concept took root in his personality, these qualities would come to be mirrored in Crane himself. At first glance, it might seem his identification with the men of action on his father's side was little more than hero-worship; but these ideals would inform much of his writing and many of his own exploits.

Crane's father, Jonathan Townley Crane, was born in 1819 and raised on a farm on the outskirts of Union, New Jersey. Orphaned early, Jonathan apprenticed with a craftsman of trunks, who would later help him to attend college. In 1843 Jonathan Crane graduated from the College of New Jersey (today's Princeton University), where he was noted for his skill in English composition. While away at college, Jonathan found that he no longer agreed with the tenets of the Presbyterianism in which he had been raised—namely, the belief in predestination, which supported the possibility of the damnation of infants. This Calvinist doctrine held that good works or acts of faith could not assure a place in heaven, that a soul either was among the "elect" and would be admitted after death or was not and would not. The rigidity of this worldview ran counter to Jonathan's emotional makeup and to his own thinking on the matter, and he soon adopted Methodism, whose creed was closely based in the Lutheran assumption that true salvation came through individual faith alone, and not by a predetermination from God that allowed no human intercession.

After his graduation, Jonathan Crane felt his calling was to become a clergyman, so he took to the road as an itinerant preacher, traveling through parts of New Jersey, Pennsylvania, and New York. While in Pennsylvania, he met Mary Helen Peck, the only daughter of Reverend George Peck of the Methodist church in Wilkes-Barre. An author, George Peck served as editor of the influential magazine *Christian Advocate*, and had published several religious works of his own. Jonathan and the 21-year-old Helen (as she was called by friends and family) were married on January 8, 1848. Helen was both educated and strong-willed; although it was then uncommon for women to achieve any higher education, in the year preceding her marriage Helen had graduated from Rutgers Female Institute in New York.

On the maternal side of Crane's family, many of the males had joined the clergy, and Jesse Truesdale Peck, Helen's uncle, was a Methodist Episcopal bishop. Bishop Peck was the pastor of the Methodist church in Syracuse and one of the founders of Syracuse University, where Crane would briefly study. In the main, Crane's affection didn't extend to the members of this side of his family as it did to those of his father's side. In a letter to a friend, he described the Pecks being so regimented that ". . . every[one] as soon as he could walk, became a Methodist clergy[man]—of the old ambling-nag, saddlebag, exhorting kind." [Davis, 5]

Jonathan and Helen quickly settled into married life. Letters during their first year reveal a devoted couple that could not bear to be separated.

Serving in the ministry meant frequent moves, and the Cranes lived in a number of communities in New Jersey and New York, staying at each post for a few years at most. Children were born with regularity. Letters to Helen's parents were filled with accounts of the children's illnesses, accidents, and first words. She told correspondents that she faced mountains of sewing, "plenty of work, enough for two or three pairs of hands." [Davis, 7] In the midst of her household chores, Helen made forays into art. Writing to her parents, she described a picture she'd done in crayons, which her husband had praised as "finer than an oil painting." She went on to say, "I have an ardent admirer of my genius in my husband, he is very proud of my paintings and flowers." [Davis, 8] Jonathan proved to be a loving and attentive husband and father who didn't mind helping with the many children. As Helen became too busy to write letters home, Jonathan took over. In letters to his wife's family, he presented warm and humorous anecdotes about the children, revealing himself as a man with a tender manner and a gentle spirit.

Their lives were not without hardship, though; several children either died in childbirth or succumbed to illness. In all, Helen would give birth to fourteen children, six of which she would see buried. During these times, Jonathan and Helen relied heavily on their faith. "Well, God reign[s]," Crane's stalwart father wrote after the death of one of the infants, observing that ". . . in His hands we are all safe, whatever awaits us." [Davis, 10] With the death of each child, Helen grieved, even burying one under a rosebush.

In the fall of 1871, the family settled into the three-story Methodist parsonage in Newark, New Jersey, located on fashionable Mulberry Street, facing the home of the wealthiest man in the town. On November 1, Helen gave birth to her last child, a son whom they named Stephen. At the time of his birth, Helen was 45 and Jonathan 52, and because of the many infant deaths the sibling closest to Stephen Crane in age was Luther, eight years Crane's senior; the oldest was Mary Helen, 21 years older than Crane. Crane, a beautiful child with golden curls and a cherubic face, was prone to illness, and by the time he was eight months old his parents were concerned enough about his health to take him to the country, where he recovered sufficiently. For the rest of his life, Crane would fare best in rural settings.

It is worth noting at this point that recent scholarship has suggested that the Thomas Beer biography of Crane, the 1923 work to which many biographical works written since can trace their ancestry, and from which much of the current knowledge of the facts of Crane's life has been derived, may have been largely spurious. This, understandably, creates a difficult situation for the biographer; the work of sorting through the knowledge base is ongoing.

The Crane family soon moved again, certainly, from Newark to Bloomington, New Jersey, where Jonathan Crane became presiding elder of the Elizabeth District. Two years later they moved to Paterson, New Jersey, after Reverend Crane's appointment as pastor of the Cross Street Church. A short time later he was transferred again, this time to Port Jervis, New York. Remote then, Port Jervis was located at the junction of three states—New York, New Jersey, and Pennsylvania—and situated by the upper reaches of the Delaware River at the foot of the Shawangunk Mountains, east of the Appalachian plateau. This rural setting would figure prominently in Crane's life and writing as representative of the best moments of his childhood. To the north of Port Jervis lay the Catskill Mountains, where Crane, as he grew older, would spend time in hunting, fishing, and camping. The rocky, semi-alpine wilderness of this area provided the setting for his "Sullivan County Sketches".

After the birth of her last child, Helen sought activities outside the confines of her home. Deeply interested in temperance, she joined the New Jersey Women's Christian Temperance Union. Her zeal for the work took her to meetings around the Port Jervis region and out of town, and she became a respected speaker and writer for the cause. Meanwhile, Crane was left in the care of his sister Agnes, a clever and self-sacrificing person who described herself as "mother's ugly duckling." [Davis, 18] What Agnes may have lacked in beauty, though, or in integration into the family, she made up for in other capacities: her grades in school were outstanding—she would leave the school as its valedictorian—and her learning wide. Crane's closest companion, she read to him constantly, teaching him science, nature, and literature, and it was under her tutelage that he learned to read and write. Because of his many bouts of illness, Crane received no formal schooling until his ninth year. When at last his health permitted him to attend school, he advanced through two grades, easily, in six weeks, and later he would remember how this rapid advancement had pleased his father. Crane said of his father that he was "so simple and good that I often [thought] he didn't know much of anything about humanity." Jonathan Crane's kindness, even naivety, from Crane's point of view may have come of a nature that was decent but sometimes lacked purview: Crane wrote that the good pastor never "drove a horse faster than two yards an hour even if some Christian was dying elsewhere." [Stallman, 7]

In the 1870s, members of what was called the "Holiness Movement" gained influence over the Methodist church community, claiming the necessity of a second conversion if one was to receive "entire sanctification." Reverend Crane, who disagreed with this position, wrote a book in 1874 condemning the movement. As a result, he found himself at odds with the emergent faction, and Helen said of this time that the upheaval in the Church conflicted with Jonathan's basic makeup and that the fact "that brethren should so differ was painful to him." [Davis, 11] His father-in-law's position in the church protected him for a while, but when Reverend Peck died, in 1876, Reverend Crane was reassigned to a small church in Paterson, New Jersey. Two years later, after receiving a salary much lower than was originally promised, the Reverend moved his family again, back to Port Jervis.

Despite the change in circumstances for the Crane family and the uncertainty of Jonathan Crane's position, this post came as a welcome reprieve from the power struggles within the Methodist Church. The entire family, especially Helen Crane, took to the quiet rural setting of Port Jervis. Soon after Jonathan assumed the pastorate, Helen began to draw large audiences to her lively lectures. She spoke out on the dangers of alcoholism, but she also presented lectures on life in foreign lands, using the town's children (and her own) as models, dressing them in the colorful costumes of the regions on which she spoke.

Crane's early years were filled with the considerable presence of his parents as both passionate speakers and persuasive writers; this may have led to his decision to become a writer himself. His father, for example, was known to write, without fail, ten pages each day in addition to his sermons, letters, and journal articles. He penned and published several tales for children, each elaborating on a particular lesson or moral. Two of Helen's folk stories, gleaned from her many lectures, appeared in the *New Jersey Tribune* and the *Monmouth Tribune*. Although Crane's uncle Jesse Peck spoke out against reading novels, and his father condemned the harmful effects of what he called "trashy literature," Crane, by way of his older brothers, had access to many dime-store publications. [Davis, 14] By the time he was seven, he had read books by James Fenimore Cooper and other popular writers, evidently with no adverse comment from his father.

A SLANT OF SUN ON A BROWN WALL

In mid-February of 1880, Crane's father made a trip to Newark with his daughter Agnes to find employment for a boy he had befriended. While away, he fell ill with a fever. Upon his return to Port Jervis, the elder Crane took to his bed with a severe cold. On Sunday the 15th, with a high fever, he ascended the pulpit without fail to preach to what Crane remembered as an "unusually large congregation." [Davis, 15] On the following day, climbing the stairs to his study to work on a sermon for an upcoming service, he collapsed, suffering extreme chest pains; he died before a doctor could be summoned. Jonathan Crane was 60 years old, and Stephen, his youngest son, had yet to reach adolescence. The *Port Jervis Daily Union* reported that those who attended Reverend Crane's funeral made up "one of the largest, if not the largest, [group of mourners] ever assembled in the church." [Davis, 16] The loss of this beloved pastor affected the entire town.

Stephen Crane was inconsolable, and the funeral clearly marks the genesis of a bitterness toward the trappings of religion—the tendency of ritual to reaffirm delusions, solely to placate the living, creating in the process a host of other problems. "We tell kids," Crane wrote, "that heaven is just across the gaping grave and all that bosh and then we scare them to glue with flowers and white sheets and hymns. We ought to be crucified for it! I have forgotten nothing about this, not a damned iota, not a shred." [Stallman, 8]

The death uprooted the family. The three oldest sons still living at home—Edmund, Wilbur, and Luther—had to leave Centenary Collegiate Institute, as their mother and siblings now had to vacate the Port Jervis parsonage. Crane's mother relocated the family to Roseville, near Newark, leaving Crane in the care of his brother Edmund, then 22. In the following summer, the eldest son, William, who had graduated from law school, took both Crane and their mother into his home in Port Jervis. Three years later, Stephen and Helen Crane moved again, this time to Asbury Park, New Jersey. It was noted by all that the loss of his father and the destabilization of the family were a considerable strain on young Crane, the only living Crane child not even to have reached adolescence by the time of its occurrence; but Crane never spoke of his experience of this period.

In the late 1800s, Asbury Park and its sister town, Ocean Grove, were Methodist seaside resorts, often the sites of exuberant camp meetings. A "dry" town that prohibited the sale of alcohol, it was advertised as "the Summer Mecca of American Methodists"; visitors were welcomed to Bible studies, temperance meetings, lectures, and concerts. Although money was scarce for Helen Crane, she managed to fund her sons' schooling from coal mine stocks she had inherited from her father. Crane's brother Townley was a reporter for the *Newark Advertiser*, which operated a summer news agency for the *New York Tribune* and the Associated Press. Both Helen Crane and her son Wilbur became contributing writers for the agency, reporting on the religious activities taking place along the Jersey shore. Crane attended school where his sister Mary Helen worked as an art instructor. Agnes soon joined them in Asbury Park, teaching at the same school. While the Crane family remained close, the town of Asbury Park offered neither the warmth nor the quietude of Port Jervis.

Crane's mother expanded her work with the Women's Christian Temperance Union (WCTU), even entertaining the organization's national leader, Frances Willard, in the Crane home. Under Willard's leadership, the organization took on a number of social causes, such as education for poor children, women's suffrage, and the organization of labor unions. Soon after their arrival in Asbury Park, Crane's mother was elected president of the local WCTU chapter. She threw herself into her new position with enthusiasm. Crane recalled how his mother began to act "more of a Christian than a Methodist"; once, she drew the wrath of the Church when she dared to take an unmarried, pregnant girl into her home to look after her. [Stallman, 9]

A few years after his father's death, Crane experienced another series of family losses. The first was Townley's wife, Fannie, whom the family had known since her childhood. Two of Townley's children also died, before or after the loss of Fannie. Then Agnes fell ill and was forced to resign her teaching position. She died of spinal meningitis on June 10, 1884 at the age of 28. Crane had just turned 12 when Agnes, his caretaker, confidant and closest sister, died, and of this he said, he suffered "one of the greatest losses of [his] life." [Sufrin, 17] With Agnes gone and his mother's energies so fully occupied, Crane had a great deal of freedom, roaming the town and frequenting nearby beaches, where he'd play baseball and football with friends. He was given a retired circus pony as a gift, which he named Pudgy, and on Pudgy he rode for hours up and down the beaches, exploring the sand dunes and the woods nearby. He was in the habit of grandstanding before the other children by riding the pony bareback into the surf.

After Agnes's death, Crane had greater contact with his older brothers, and this had an immediate effect on him, for in great contrast to both Agnes and Helen Crane the brothers were worldly and secular. "I used to like church and prayer meeting when I was a kid," Crane later recalled, "but that cooled off and when I was thirteen or about that, my brother Will told me not to believe in Hell after my uncle had been boring me about the Lake of Fire and the rest of those sideshows." [Sufrin, 18] Indeed—perhaps from the cumulative effect of his recent losses and the influence of his older brothers—Crane began to rebel openly against the Methodist worldview of his immediate family.

Beyond riding his pony, Crane enjoyed playing baseball with the Asbury Park school team, and he proved to be an outstanding athlete. He shared with his mother his ideas of becoming a professional baseball player; she put her foot down; Crane wrote to a friend of that she had called baseball "not a serious occupation" and that "Will says I have to go to college first." [Sufrin, 18]

At this time, when he was approximately 13 years old, Crane's talent for writing began to surface. An essay he wrote won him a prize of twenty-five cents. His "Uncle Jake and the Bell-Handle"—his first story, exploring the mishaps of a farmer who visits the city for the first time—also dates to these years. "Uncle Jake" demonstrates an early, basic understanding of plot, dialogue, and the development of characters. The narrative follows the events that occur after the farmer accidentally pulls a bell-handle—that, unknown to him, summons the fire department—and is harassed on all sides by various residents of the town. On September 14, 1885, two months before his fourteenth birthday, Crane's mother enrolled him at the Methodist seminary school in Pennington, New Jersey. The school, where his father had served as principal, was highly orthodox. Services were held twice daily in the school's chapel, and Sunday morning services were held in one of the two churches in the village. Bible classes were held on Sunday afternoons and prayer meetings every Wednesday evening. Crane's carefree days at Asbury Park were over, it seemed, as he was required to attend all these services. Yet, in spite of the pious atmosphere at Pennington and his doubts about Methodism, Crane remained at the school for two and a half years without known incident.

During his first year at Pennington, Crane's mother suffered a breakdown. Because of her prominence in the community, the Asbury Park *Shore News* reported that she was "suffering from a temporary aberration of the mind" and "in a critical condition"—while a rival paper, the Asbury Park *Journal*, wrote, "[T]hough her mind is yet feeble it is hoped with returning strength her mental troubles will disappear." [Stallman, 569] There is no mention in Crane's letters or journals of how her condition affected him. The following fall, a train hit Crane's brother Luther, a flagman for the Erie Railroad. Taken to William's house, Luther died within twenty-four hours of the accident. Again, there is no record of Crane's reaction; but in this latter case some assumptions are appropriate.

Following an altercation with one of his teachers, Crane left Pennington in the middle of his third year, and his mother sent him to Claverack College and Hudson River Institute in New York State. The school, originally founded by Methodists, had been all but absorbed by a military school, and its standards hardly conformed to the school's religious origins. Many of the boys at Claverack came from families with "backward or semi-incorrigible offspring." [Davis, 24] One of Crane's classmates, Harvey Wickham, would later describe the school as a place where boys and girls "roamed as if in a terrestrial paradise like packs of cheerful wolves out of bounds, out [at all] hours and very much out of hand." [Sufrin, 20] Crane spent some of the happiest years of his life there, calling it a "bully time" and "simply pie." By his own admittance, he didn't learn a thing from his classes; but he had a marvelous time playing baseball. While still at Asbury Park school, he had already established himself as a good barehanded catcher, and at Claverack he began to use a buckskin glove, which prevented sprains and injuries while improving his abilities. The school didn't have uniforms, so the boys wore whatever clothing they had, giving them the "appearance of Joseph in the Bible . . . with his coat of many colors." [Stallman, 19]

Crane struggled with mathematics and the sciences, but he was far advanced in history and literature. Owing largely to the efforts of his sister Agnes, he was well acquainted with American and English poets and could readily quote verses or, more often, complete poems. Friends remembered that Crane always had his face in a book, reading a novel or a Greek classic. About his military obligations Crane was scrupulous, and he was promoted quickly to the rank of corporal. To his subordinates, he was at once a mother hen and a strict disciplinarian. A photograph of him in his school uniform shows a solemn young man with steady eyes and close-cropped, neatly parted hair. There can be little doubt that Crane's interest in war and the military was fostered by his activities at Claverack. In the summer, Crane returned to Asbury Park, where he set about gathering news for his widowed brother Townley, who had become known as a tenacious reporter. Crane's position was not a formal hiring by the *Tribune*; rather, his brother paid him out of pocket for the unsigned pieces he submitted. Crane later noted that relatives all but obscured his presence in Asbury Park, that he was merely the kid brother running errands and gathering news items.

Back at Claverack, Crane was becoming an enigma to his friends, developing a dual nature. On one hand, his manner was undisciplined and sloppy: he cut classes to play baseball and cared little about doing his homework, was known for frequenting billiard rooms, smoked incessantly, and swore frequently. On the other hand, he refused to join in any pranks that might cause real harm, for he took no pleasure in abusing others. His crowd was the wealthier students, even though he often wore baggy pants and a dirty, tattered sweater. He joined with a group of boys to form a secret misogynist society while falling madly in love with several of his female classmates. Crane went out of his way to befriend a group of Cuban students enrolled at Claverack while the other boys ignored or harassed them. Later, the little Spanish he had learned from them would be of use during his days as a Cuban war correspondent and in Mexico.

His classmate Wickham described Crane's personality at the time as "self-deprecation coupled with arrogance." Tommie Borland called Crane "a law unto himself." [Davis, 26] As for his writing: Crane saw two of his essays published in the school paper, the *Vidette*. Also, the Reverend General John

Bullock Van Petten, a Civil War veteran and Crane's history teacher, told vivid war stories in the classroom, and his account of Antietam in particular impressed Crane to such an extent that Crane would later include elements of it in *The Red Badge of Courage*.

While Crane was living agreeably at Claverack, though, his mother and brother William were discussing his future. It was decided, mainly by William, that there was no future in a military career, and as the family owned shares in a mining venture mining became the obvious choice. Helen enrolled Crane at Lafayette College in Easton, Pennsylvania for the upcoming semester. Although he was greatly saddened and disappointed to leave, he put on an air of nonchalance as he said good-bye to school friends, letting them think he had tired of Claverack; in truth, although he may well have tired of his classes, he would miss his friends and all he had experienced there. In the summer of 1890, Crane again worked with Townley at the paper, this time seeing his byline in print. His other had just published two humorous stories and one historical account of Ocean Grove's oldest house. She also had successfully submitted one of Agnes's short stories for publication. Crane was surrounded by family members in publishing.

When he arrived at Lafayette in the fall, he found a school with a curriculum that was almost the opposite of Claverack's. With no electives offered, he faced grueling lectures in algebra, chemistry, and French. Making an attempt to become a part of the social scene, he joined the fraternity Delta Upsilon and took part in its traditional hike to the summit of mount Paxinosa. Hazing, an integral and not strictly forbidden school tradition, took place not only in the fraternities but between classes as well. The sophomores hazed the freshmen with a vengeance. Crane lived alone in a room in East Hall, where he waited in fear for something to happen. On one memorable occasion, when upperclassmen arrived to break open his locked door, they saw in the dim lamplight a white-faced Crane holding a loaded revolver. Crane dropped the revolver, also in fear; but no hazing took place in his room on that night. This was one of the few times in Crane's life when he would lose his nerve. Shortly after this night, while taking part in the annual tug-of-war between freshmen and sophomores, he reveled in having seized the flag from the senior class—possibly foreshadowing a scene in *The Red Badge of Courage*. Sending the flag to his friend Odell Hathaway at Claverack, he wrote:

> It doesn't look like much does it? Only an old rag, ain't it? But you remember I got a black and blue nose, a barked shin, skin off my hands and a lame shoulder, in the row; you can appreciate. So, keep it, and when you look at it think of me scrapping about

twice a week over some old rag that says 'Fresh '94' on it.
[Stallman, 25]

Because his goal was to make the varsity baseball team in the following
spring, he took part in intramural games nearly every afternoon during the
fall. The rest of his spare time was spent in a poolroom behind a tobacco
store in Easton. Out of seven courses he received grades in four, two of which
were failing. For the remaining three, he received no grades at all, for he had
never attended class. After the Christmas holidays, Crane returned to the
school long enough to pack up and leave. He said little to anyone except that
family problems prevented his return. The truth was that he had failed out;
and had this not been the case, he would have left anyway. "I found mining
engineering not at all to my taste," he said of this time. "I preferred baseball."
[Sufrin, 27] His next and final attempt at formal education was at Syracuse
University in New York. Again, his family played a substantial part in this
choice; since his great-uncle Bishop Peck had founded the school, his
acceptance into this institution was all but guaranteed. In the meantime, his
brother Townley got him a job as a Syracuse correspondent for the *New York
Tribune*. Upon his arrival, Crane boarded with his great-aunt, but his stay was
short-lived. He moved into the Delta Upsilon frat house as soon as a room
was available. There his living habits produced a room strewn with tobacco
cans, pipes, newspapers, unwashed clothing, and books.

Syracuse, a large city with many seedy areas to explore, filled Crane
with anticipation, as did the prospect of playing baseball again. "This is a
dandy city and I expect to see some fun here," he remarked. [Sufrin, 28] His
idea of fun, it can be assumed, was to mitigate the Methodist piety of his
surroundings with however he could. When the temperance leader Frances
Willard, whom he'd met through his mother, came to lecture at Syracuse, he
flatly refused to attend, calling her a fool. He held all of his professors in
contempt as well, feeling no particular allegiance to anyone's point of view,
let alone a crone in a high white collar. When an upperclassman fraternity
brother called him across the library to help sharpen knives for the kitchen,
Crane shouted back he would never turn a grindstone for anyone. Beneath
Crane's aloof demeanor lay a resoluteness not to be crossed. Baseball training
began in February, and Crane joined the team as a catcher. It was on the
baseball field, one of the few places he experienced anything that remotely
resembled joy, that he really shined. He was light on his feet and a fast base
runner. Small in stature, at 5 feet 6 inches tall and 125 pounds, he played with
grit, swearing openly and leveling sarcastic remarks on bad plays and offering
generous praise on good ones. As a consequence, he was considered one of
the best players on the team and elected captain.

Taking his role as a newspaper correspondent seriously as well, Crane spent many hours at police courts and in forbidden theaters and bars, and he skulked through the red-light district of Syracuse in search of stories. His reasoning was that police court and the red-light district offered a far better education than a university. Already a chain smoker at the age of 19, Crane tempered the ire of his fraternity brothers over the matter of the offending odors emanating from his room by successfully leading a minority group of smokers to petition for the use of an unfinished cupola atop the house where they could smoke in peace. When winter came, they simply wore scarves, earflaps, and gloves, visiting the smoking area despite even bitter weather. Burned into the wood of the east wall of the cupola: "sunset 1891 May / Steph Crane." [Stallman, 32]

During his stay at Syracuse, Crane's writing showed marked improvement. His deadpan, tongue-in-cheek article "Great Bugs of Onondaga" appeared in the *Tribune* on June 1, 1891. In addition, he allowed his friends to read the rough drafts of "a novel in progress"—the initial sketch for *Maggie: A Girl of the Streets.* On June 12, Crane attended a Delta Upsilon chapter meeting; shortly thereafter he left the school forever, saying goodbye to no one. He had failed algebra, chemistry, physics, education, and German, but he had earned an A in English literature. His performance marked the end of his formal education.

SELF-MADE MAN

Crane's brother William remained in Port Jervis, where he became a respected judge and took up residence in an expansive Victorian home on East Main Street. As a member and one of the founders of the Hartwood Club (also known as the Hartwood Park Association), Judge Crane acquired several thousand acres of land adjacent to the Club's property. The Club itself owned six thousand acres of timber and lakes, with hunting rights on most of it. Crane's parents had taken him and his siblings on camping expeditions in some of these same wilderness areas, so he was familiar with many of the bodies of water in Sullivan County, especially Eddy Pond, where once he had caught a pickerel. An avid outdoorsman, Crane was a good swimmer, accomplished with a rifle, and an expert with horses. Several of his winter vacations from school had been spent at William's house, and he loved to listen to the tales of Indian uprisings, bears, wild hogs, and panthers from the "old-timers" who lived in and around Sullivan County. In the summer of 1891, Crane, along with friends Frederic Lawrence, Louis ("Lew") Senger, and Louis Carr, decided to spend a few weeks in the back country of Sullivan County. They tramped through thickets, slept under the stars, and spent time at the homesteads of the county's older residents, who offered an oral history of the region in their tales.

Following his camping adventures, Crane returned to Asbury Park, where he took a full-time position as a correspondent for the *Tribune*. It may seem hard to imagine that Crane could bear the mundane work of reporting on the town's pleasure-seekers; however, he found the prosperous families a fascinating study in human nature. He also sought out by-the-way places where sex, gambling, and the immoderate consumption of liquor were hidden by a veneer of respectability. He liked to compare the Asbury Park poker players to those in Ocean Grove, dutifully singing doxologies as they dealt from the bottom of the deck. It was through the writing he did at the *Tribune* this time that he was able to develop a voice that was his own and a strategic sense of irony that would bring to his narratives a gruff, unsentimental clarity that resonates in much of his later works. One assignment in particular, given to Crane in August, would prove to change his professional life: A young writer from Boston named Hamlin Garland was giving a lecture at Avon-by-the-Sea, and Crane was assigned to cover the event. Garland, a teacher and a rising literary star, had published in such notable magazines as *Harper's Weekly* and *The Arena*. That morning, Garland spoke about a fellow author, William Dean Howells, and Crane was bowled over by his presentation. For not only was Garland the first professional writer he'd ever met, but Garland's discussion of the function of realism in fiction touched on some of the considerations Crane had been working in his own writing. After the lecture, the two became acquainted, finding they had many things in common, one of these being a love of baseball. The two men would talk for hours as they pitched a ball to one another on the beach. When Garland, ten years Crane's senior, left New Jersey after his final lecture, he assumed he would never see Crane again.

The allure of the underbelly of life in the city, acquired in Asbury Park and indulged through his work as correspondent at Syracuse, would become emblematic of Crane's quest for a fiction that was not only drawn from reality but also free of social or political agenda and artifice. He began making treks into the Bowery after the news agency closed down, as it did every Labor Day. New York's burgeoning population—that had more than doubled, from 500,000 to 1.1 million, between 1850 and 1880—gave birth to a new underclass of tenement dwellers, who were crammed in vast numbers into economically and socially divided neighborhoods and slums. The Bowery was a fourteen-block pocket of petty criminals, ne'er-do-wells, and prostitutes that was bordered on its southern side by Park Avenue. Many of the major newspapers in New York at the time were based in the area, so it was to this part of Manhattan Island that Crane was drawn, convinced he would never write anything true if he didn't experience the whole of life first-hand. The raw, desperate nature of life in the slums fostered in Crane an immediacy of perception that would reveal the self-satisfaction of the well-heeled at Asbury Park as not merely irresponsible, but contemptible.

In October, Crane's mother fell ill. Months earlier, she had resigned as president of the WCTU, and she had curtailed many of her other activities. She died, on December 7, 1891, at a hospital in Paterson, with only Townley at her side. This loss seems to have driven Crane deeper into the subterranean landscape of New York. Between jaunts to the Bowery, Crane made visits to his brothers for square meals and a place to sleep. They tried to dissuade him from what seemed to them a hell-bound course of life, doubtful of the benefits of this lifestyle to Crane even as a writer. Often, Crane would become impatient with what he considered their provincial attitudes and endless queries and retreat into silence. Helen, Wilbur's daughter, later remembered how her uncle was ill at ease around the family, for "when it came to gossip and inane small talk, he was sunk. . . . He just couldn't stand it and was very unpredictable in what he said." [Sufrin, 41]

Back in Asbury Park during the summer in 1892, Crane all but took over the news agency as Townley turned more and more to alcohol and poker. At 21, Crane was thoroughly familiar with the crowds of preachers, dignitaries, ingénues, entertainers, and businessmen who filled the hotels and strolled along the boardwalks. In the evenings, the electric lights flickered and brass bands played while the inhabitants showed off their finery. The town spent vast sums of money on such attractions as an athletic field and a bicycle track for the express purpose of summer amusement. That summer, Crane covered every corner of the beach, submitting dozens of articles to the *Tribune*. He befriended a fellow reporter by the name of Arthur Oliver, who, like Crane, wanted to write something memorable. "But," as Oliver explained to Crane, "I get all tangled up with different notions of how it ought to be told." To which Crane responded by throwing a handful of sand into the wind and saying, "Treat your notions like that. Forget what you think about it and tell how you feel about it. . . . That's the big secret of story telling. . . . Be yourself!" [Davis, 49]

It was also during this summer that Crane fell in love with Lily Brandon Munroe, who was married to Hersey Munroe, a wealthy man who lavished on her a home in Washington, D.C. and another in New York. Hersey Munroe, an eminent geologist, was out of the country for the summer, and his wife stayed at the Lake Avenue Hotel, in which Townley's press bureau office was located. She had blonde hair, and Crane often expressed a preference for women of her physical type. In the beginning, she was able to overlook Crane's frail build and hacking cough, his unkempt appearance, and his intense, melancholic nature. She saw him as "extremely brilliant" and "very idealistic, without a trace of vulgarity." [Davis, 47] She was especially attracted, it seems, to Crane's "remarkable" eyes. Delighted to give the town gossips something to talk about, Crane often appeared in public with Munroe on his arm, strolling the boardwalks, riding the carousel, eating ice cream, and watching the waves roll in on the beach. The two fell in love, and Crane wanted to marry Munroe, but her father was, understandably, intensely opposed to the idea. Mr. Brandon put his foot down on meeting Crane in New York, observing how uncultivated and poverty-stricken he appeared. Eventually, Crane asked Munroe to elope with him; after serious consideration, she declined. Later, her husband found out about them and destroyed the letters and pictures Crane had given to her.

On August 17, 1892, the American Day parade of the Junior Order of United American Mechanics took place on the streets of Asbury Park—an event that would bring infamy on Crane. Crane and his reporter friend Arthur Oliver were smoking cigars in a billiard parlor when they noticed the laborers of the Mechanics' Union assembling on the street, carrying banners; they ran out to learn what was happening. Steadfastly and imperviously, they pushed past the stunned patrons of nearby seaside resorts and upscale hotels, who were completely taken aback by the procession. The contradictory nature of this display—the class-consciousness of it—appealed to Crane's sensibilities as a journalist, so he hurried back to the *Tribune* office to write down what he had seen. His article, appearing in the features section on the following Sunday and ironically entitled "On the Jersey Coast—Parades and Entertainments," caused an uproar in the Asbury Park community. Contrasting the prim summer costumes of the onlookers with the parade of Mechanics dressed in the garb of their trade, he described the marchers:

> . . . not seeming to quite understand, stolid, unconcerned and, in a certain sense, dignified—a pace and a bearing emblematic of their lives. They smiled occasionally and from time to time greeted friends in the crowd on the sidewalk. Such an assemblage of the *spraddle-legged* men of the middle class, whose hands were bent and shoulders stooped from delving and constructing, had never appeared to an Asbury Park summer crowd, and the latter was vaguely amused. [Stallman, 54]

The intent of the article was entirely misconstrued, especially by members of the Mechanics' Union, who wrote to the editor in protest of the piece, saying it was un-American to criticize a body of brothers bound together "to honor and protect [their] country." Crane was accused of sneering at the union members for their appearance and for marching. As demands were made for an apology, Townley jumped to the defense of his brother lamenting, the fact that a correspondent had no right "to say anything about the town excepting in the way of praise." [Davis, 50] Unfortunately, politics played more of a part in the upheaval than did the words of the article. Whitelaw Reid, not only the owner of the *Tribune* but also a Republican candidate for vice-president of the United States, was outraged. Rival Democratic papers were the first to cry out that the American worker had been insulted. Yet had the piece been read more carefully, it would have been clear that the onlookers bore the greater insult. On August 24, the *Tribune* issued an apology without naming Crane as the author, calling the article a "bit of random correspondence, inadvertently [overlooked] by the copy editor." [Davis, 50]

Crane and Townley both were promptly fired. Their brother William would later say that the firing made a broken man of Townley. It had just the opposite effect on Crane; the whole incident was amusing to him. Arthur Oliver remembered that Townley looked "glum as a king who had lost his crown," whereas Crane greeted Oliver "with [the] saintly smile he always had for every disaster." Some time later, when asked whether he regretted writing the article, he replied, "No! You've got to feel the things you write if you want to make an impact on the world." [Davis, 51]

THE OMINOUS BABY

In 1870, a Danish man by the name of Jacob Riis immigrated to the United States and settled in New York City. After years of extreme poverty, he found work as a police reporter for the *New York Tribune* in 1877. Moved by the squalor of the tenements (with an estimated population of 37,000 people at the time), he began carrying a camera with him, snapping photos of the conditions he found in ramshackle buildings and alleys strewn with the refuse of lives spent toiling in sweatshops and foundries. The candid reporting and graphic depictions of the squalor of the New York poor in his *How the Other Half Lives: Studies Among the Tenements of New York* (1890) shocked the nation. Originating a new kind of documentary photography, Riis photographed the hollow eyes of children who worked twelve hours or more a day in mills and of adults of every nationality who braved deadly working conditions to bring home a wage that often wasn't enough to feed their families. While the pictures alone were enough to play upon the readers' sympathies, his incendiary social critique would inspire reforms that would affect the lives of millions of people. In 1892, Riis gave a lecture at Avon-by-the-Sea, and Crane attended. While he gave no sign of being influenced by the reformer, Crane did, after a fashion, follow in his footsteps, by depicting the lives of the "other half" in fictional accounts and sketches.

In the fall of that year, Crane rented in an apartment between the Bowery and the East River in one of New York's notorious ghettoes. Other residents of the building included a group of medical students and two of Crane's old friends, Frederic Lawrence and Lucius Button, who called the place the *Pendennis Club*. Donning ragged clothes, Crane set out to explore side streets of the tenement districts, with their two-cent restaurants, opium dens, dive bars, and whorehouses. Then he'd return to the crowded apartment, with fresh encounters lingering in his head, and sit down to write. Out of the window of his apartment was a view of the East River and the prison yard at Blackwell's Island. Such scenes appeared in his manuscript:

> From a window of an apartment house that up rose from amid squat, ignorant stables, there leaned a curious woman. Some laborers, unloading a scow at a dock at the river, paused for a moment . . . The engineer of a passive tugboat hung lazily over a railing and watched. Over on the Island, a worm of yellow convicts came from the shadow of a grey ominous building and crawled slowly over the river's bank. [Davis, 55]

Crane's manuscript, like the photographs of Riis, focused on the effects of poverty on the inhabitants of the New York slums. Earlier examples of this type of character study had been penned by writers like Horatio Alger, who glossed over the tragic aspects of his characters, supporting the ideal of "the American Dream" through his rags-to-riches tales of "Ragged Dick" and showing how with the right attitude the exploited could rise above their degradation. Crane took no such path. Instead, he wrote about the hardships that befell people in real life, in a seemingly indifferent universe, and this tone permeated his characters. What he offered the reader would be neither a happy ending nor a convenient explanation, but visceral portrayals that were unbiased and often unrelenting. While he told a friend there was no preaching in his book, he had in fact made strong statements on every page— implicating all but the main character for her downfall. In the first draft, his characters had no names. Later, when encouraged by his brother William and others to name his characters to prevent confusion, he named his protagonist Maggie. Townley introduced Crane to Richard Watson Gilder, the editor of the magazine *Century*, who subsequently read the manuscript. Gilder felt it too harsh and rejected it. He later recalled the young man sitting in his office as thin and pale, wrapped in an Ulster much too large for him, and that Crane's "blue eyes seemed enormous." [Stallman, 67]

A friend of Crane's from Asbury Park, Wallis McHarg, visited him in New York before setting off for Europe. Given the manuscript to read, McHarg thought it new, outlandish, and strange, and he told Crane he doubted that any publisher would print it. Indeed, one publisher after another rejected the manuscript. Turning for advice to Willis Johnson, editor of the *Tribune*, Crane was told that *Maggie* was just too coarse for the general public. "It would so shock the Podsnaps and Mrs. Grundys as to bring him a storm of condemnation." [Davis, 56]

The winter of 1892 was difficult for Crane. Although he had seen his first work published in a popular magazine, he lacked funds most of the time. He wrote to a friend, offering to "sell [his] steps to the grave at ten cents per foot." [Davis, 57] Regarding *Maggie*, Crane saw no recourse but to publish it himself. In January of 1893, he had the book copyrighted at the Library of Congress; he then sold his rights to his mother's mining shares to William for about $1,000—the approximate equivalent of $18,000 in 2001—and, using this money, hired a printer without even discussing price. (He would later learn that he had been charged $700 more in publishing fees than was common at the time.) Under the pseudonym of *Johnston Smith*, the book was released in March of 1893 for sale at the modest price of fifty cents per copy. No bookstore or newsstand would accept it, though, for the contents were simply too graphic and controversial. Crane was crushed, having naively thought that once people actually read the book rave reviews would follow, and then he would appear and take a bow as the work's author. Instead, he found himself giving copies away just to make room in the apartment. "Poor Maggie!" he lamented. "She was one of my first loves." [Sufrin, 56]

When the writer Hamlin Garland acquired a copy of the book and learned that Crane was the author, he immediately sent it to William Dean Howells. Both men were impressed by the art, the energy, and the power behind the work. Garland wrote a glowing review of *Maggie*, which appeared in the literary magazine *Arena*. Howells invited Crane to attend a luncheon, at which he found himself surrounded by many noted authors of the New York literary community. Howells, in his mid-fifties, was intrigued by the young writer, describing him as a "strange, melancholy beauty . . . [with an] ironical smile . . . [and] mystical, clouded eyes." [Davis, 62] Howells used his influence to persuade bookstores to carry *Maggie*, and for ministers interested in reform to read it. When even Howells' influence brought about no change, though, Crane's ire against the New York literary establishment grew intense. Critics who now knew the identity of the author acknowledged his abilities, but they flinched at the brutalities in the book. The dichotomy confused Crane. In a letter to Lily Munroe, he wrote, "They tell me I did a horrible thing, but, they say, 'it's great.'" [Davis, 62]

In January of 1893, Crane followed his friend Lew Senger to the apartment of Senger's cousin, the painter Corwin Knapp Linson. A few years older than Crane, "C.K." Linson had studied art in Europe. He and Crane warmed to each other immediately, after which Crane spent many hours at Linson's brick apartment house in Chelsea. While Linson busied himself with his canvases, Crane rummaged through old Civil War issues of *Century* magazine. The Civil War tales of his youth, the legendary exploits of his father's ancestors, and the influence of his days at Claverack combined to engender in Crane a fascination with the drills, battle strategies, transmissions of orders, meals of hardtack and coffee, and knapsacks and gear of each soldier, but he noticed what he considered a major lack: the magazines described little or nothing of the soldiers' own experience of the battles. At one point, Crane threw a magazine down in frustration and said, "They spout eternally of what they *did*, but they are emotionless as rocks." [Davis, 63] As he pored over the magazines, a plot began to form in Crane's mind. Because he was without funds, his first thought was to turn out a potboiler to make a quick profit. But as the story grew, he knew it would be much more. His idea was to portray what it felt like to be in the middle of a battle as bullets whizzed past, cannon fired, and wounded soldiers shrieked through the dust and smoke that hovered in the air. As he began to write, his ideas flowed onto the paper effortlessly. Not having to consider any specific historical incidents, the narrative seemed to produce itself.

In the fall of 1893, Crane, along with some artists, moved into a studio apartment in the old Art Students' League building on East 23rd Street. He had little money for rent, and consequently he ate only infrequently. While three of the men shared a double bed, a fourth slept on a cot. They shared their meager food and clothing. The financially disastrous Panic of 1893 had hit; some 15,000 companies went out of business in that year, and while Crane lived in the League building thousands nationwide were hungry and out of work. Despite this, Frederick Gordon remembered that although their meals were scant or nonexistent they remained "free, gay, [and] hard working." [Davis, 74] Crane was very much at home in the dilapidated building with his friends, whom he called "the Indians," as he penned much of what would become *The Red Badge of Courage* cramped in a corner of the apartment. The others were impressed by his meticulous handwriting and his unshakable concentration. Since he couldn't afford a typewriter—a recent invention at the time—he explained to them the reason for such precision was to make it easier for typesetters to read his manuscript. If a revision was necessary, his practice was carefully to rewrite the entire page.

Continually without funds, Crane made contact with Edward Marshall, Sunday editor of the *New York Press*, to ask whether Marshall would take him on as a reporter. At the time, Crane was without shoes and usually wore a pair rubber boots. However, for his trip to the editor's office, he gathered enough money to buy an inexpensive pair of thin-soled shoes. Marshall told him he would pay him five dollars for every article he turned in, to which he added encouragingly, ". . . [Y]ou are made for better things. Don't waste your time." [Sufrin, 63] He had read *Maggie*, and he kindly offered some suggestions. Upon leaving, being too proud to mention he lacked a nickel for carfare, Crane walked home without a coat in freezing rain, and subsequently he fell ill. Feeling sorry for his friend, Frederick Gordon put Crane up in his own apartment for a week, until he recovered. With the little money he earned writing sketches for Marshall, Crane was able to afford shelter while working on the manuscript.

Hamlin Garland took pity on Crane as well, and in February sent him to talk with S. S. McClure, editor of *McClure Magazine*, with a stern message to McClure not to leave him waiting in the lobby for an hour. Because of the attention of men such as Garland and McClure, Crane wrote a letter to Lily Munroe, bragging how he would be leaving on an assignment to Europe very soon (which wasn't true), closing the letter with a pledge of undying love. Concomitantly with the manuscript, Crane worked on a collection poems during the cold days of February. Linson and his artist friend Émile Stangé were struck by Crane's use of color and texture in his poems. When Linson asked Crane how he came about them, he pointed to his head and said, "They came and I wrote them, that's all." [Stallman, 88] "The Indians" at the Artist's League, however, were less than sympathetic. Poking fun at the poems, they taunted him without restraint. "They think my lines are funny," he told Howells, ". . . [they made] a circus of me." [Stallman, 89] Crane would get his comeuppance by making less than salutary caricatures of them in a later novel.

On February 26, a blizzard rolled through New York, burying the city in a foot and a half of snow in less than thirty hours. Strong winds billowed down the corridors between buildings, and traffic was snarled in almost every direction. Having previously been encouraged by Garland to write about the city breadlines—since the city made much of their feeding of the poor—Crane chose this day to investigate. Out in the storm with Linson, they stood in one of the cities breadlines wearing neither coats nor headgear observing the unfortunates who waited in line for a thin concoction that would barely take the chill from a person's nose. The next day, Linson visited the apartment and found Crane exhausted, feverishly writing in nothing more than an undershirt. When asked why he had not put more on, Crane replied, "How would I know how those poor devils felt if I was warm myself? Nit! Anyway, I didn't have the shirts, you mutt!" [Stallman, 94] From this

experience, Crane wrote "Men in the Storm" and "Experiment in Misery"—
which two works, when published, placed his name before the newspaper
public for the first time. The same month these articles appeared in the *Press*,
Crane completed his war novel. First entitled *Private Fleming, His Various
Battles*, this book would thrust him into the spotlight.

EXPERIMENTAL MISERY

By the spring of 1894, the name Stephen Crane kept popping up in literary
circles across New York. John Barry, editor of *Focus* read from Crane's poetry
at a meeting of the Uncut Leaves Society—a meeting held to honor author
Frances Hodgson Burnett. William Dean Howells often talked about Crane
with close friends such as Samuel Clemens (Mark Twain), Sarah Orne Jewett,
George W. Cable and his friend Hamlin Garland. Excerpts of *Maggie*
appeared in *The New York Press* along with the comments that the work
contained "the kind of truth that no American has ever had the courage (or
is it bravado?), to put between book covers before." [Davis, 84] In April, a
gaunt, malnourished Crane showed up at Garland's door with a large
manuscript. When asked if the writing was more poetry, Crane answered,
"No, it is a tale." [Stallman, 92] While Crane wolfed down a steak cooked by
Garland's brother Franklin, he read the manuscript of *The Red Badge of
Courage*, which he said immediately "took him captive." Garland could
hardly connect the writing in his hands to the thin, pale man whom sat at his
kitchen table. "I experienced the thrill . . . of the editor who has fallen
unexpectedly upon the work of genius. It was if the youth in some mysterious
way had secured the cooperation of a spirit, the spirit of an officer in the Civil
War." [Stallman, 93] When Crane was asked how he came to know so much
about battle and war, he answered that it had been gained on the football
field. When he finished the partial manuscript he demanded to read the
remainder. Embarrassed, Crane admitted it was in hock to a typist he owed
fifteen dollars. Graciously, Garland loaned him the money saying that
everyone had to borrow from time to time and not to worry about it.
However, Crane was destined to want for most his short life. After reading
the entire manuscript, Garland contacted as many of his editor friends as
possible telling him about Crane's talents. As he had done previously,
Garland sent Crane to S.S. McClure who took the manuscript to read.

 While on summer vacation at his brother's home in Port Jervis, Corwin
Linson came to relay a message from McClure that the he wanted Crane to
write a series of articles on coal mines, and that he had hired Linson to do
the illustrations. He readily accepted the assignment, and after only two
journeys into a pit, Crane wrote an incredible sketch entitled "In the Depths

of a Coal Mine." In it, he described the drop of the elevator where the "dead black walls slide swiftly by . . . a swirling dark chaos on which the mind tried vainly to locate some coherent thing, some intelligible spot." [Stallman, 111] They were led deep into a shaft down passageways so small they were forced to crawl. Crane described the miner's faces hard and desperate, blackened not only by soot but also by the meager wages they earned. There were boys of "spanking age" who worked as slate pickers, and a mule named "China," that he learned had not been above ground for four years. In this essay, he made no bones about pointing out that only the greedy coal-brokers profited one from the mines. The piece that was published in *McClure Magazine* disgusted Crane, after he discovered McClure had made extensive edits to the manuscript, radically changing the tone of essay he submitted. "The birds didn't want the truth after all . . ." he wrote, "Why the hell did they send me up there then? So they want the public to think the coal-mines gilded ball-rooms with the miners eating ice-cream in boiled shirt-fronts?" [Stallman, 112]

Having completed the mine piece, Crane returned to Port Jervis much to the delight of the nieces of his brother's William and Edmund. He joined in their games, the girls becoming a band of outlaws and Crane the sheriff in pursuit. Heedless of the neighbors who shot disapproving glances in his direction that a full-grown man would encourage such antics, Crane went right on playing in the spirit of Twain's character *Huck Finn*, who loved nothing more than to "ruffle the skirts" of small town busy bodies. He drank the fresh lemonade his nieces concocted and ate the bread they baked, complementing them for every thing they did. William's daughter Edna in her memoirs, "My Uncle, Stephen Crane, as I Knew Him," noted the only time he wouldn't dote on them was when he'd donned his white trousers to go play tennis with the young ladies, or when he was sitting in the rocking chair on the porch writing. The girls were instructed by their mothers to leave their uncle alone while he worked. All the nieces, and their many friends, adored him.

Toward the end of the summer, Linson returned to Port Jervis for an outing at Camp Interlaken in the Twin Lakes region of the Hudson River Valley. Here Crane and his friends devised a mock newspaper, which they dubbed the "Pike County Puzzle." The contents show a clever and humorous side, that surface periodically, especially, as Linson observed, when Crane was in the country. He was happy "as a colt let loose in pasture. . . . The freedom of the woods and the youthful horseplay of the land and water sports were good medicine [for him]." [Stallman, 116] In the evenings, Crane strummed a guitar and serenaded his friends with his tenor voice. But the summer wasn't completely without frustration, though. His collection of poems lay in the hands of Copeland & Day Publishing, and they contacted Crane saying they wanted only some of the poems he submitted for the book, and requested that he write new ones to replace the ones they'd cut. After a good deal of haggling, the poems were finally accepted for publication under the title, *The Black Riders and Other Lines*. As was his habit, Crane returned to New York in the fall taking a room near the Art Student's League. It had been six months since McClure took *The Red Badge of Courage* manuscript, and Crane's patience grew thin. The truth was, McClure would have published *The Red Badge of Courage*, but he had overspent on his magazine and couldn't afford a large project such as a novel—that was part of the reason he sent Crane on assignment to the coal mines—to stall for time.

Fed up, Crane turned to his new friend Edward Marshall for advice. Marshall suggested taking the work to Irving Bacheller of the Bacheller-Johnson Newspaper Syndicate. Bacheller had already heard about Crane and was willing to read the manuscript. Bacheller would recount later how he and his wife stayed up most of the night reading it aloud to one another. He sent for Crane the next morning offering to serialize the novel. This venture was purely experimental since the syndicate never used pieces of its length; however, Bacheller was willing to take that risk. Thankfully, his editors agreed with him, but it would have to be shortened from 55,000 words to 18,000. To Crane, this was better than nothing, as it had been a long year for him with very little income, but now things were beginning to fall into place. Short stories were being accepted, newspaper work came to him, a book of poetry was scheduled for release and now *The Red Badge of Courage* would appear before the public in December. Segments of the novel first appeared in the *Philadelphia Press*, the *Kansas City Star*, the *Nebraska State Journal*, the *Minneapolis Tribune*, and the Sunday edition of the *New York Press*. In spite of the constricted version, the appearance of *The Red Badge of Courage* made quite a stir across the country. A notice in the *Philadelphia Press* said:

> If you have not been reading "The Red Badge of Courage," by Stephen Crane, the story which has been running in "The Press" for three or four days, you have been missing one of the best war stories going. Stephen Crane is a new name now and unknown, but everybody will be talking about him if he goes on as he has begun. [Davis, 95]

The editor of the *Philadelphia Press* urged Bacheller to bring Crane to their offices so they could meet him. When Crane arrived at the building, he was surprised to be surrounded by proofreaders, reporters, editors and compositors, all of whom wanted to meet him and shake his hand—this was his first blush of fame.

But Crane was by no means satisfied with the syndication of his book. His desire was to eventually see it in book form in its entirety. Feeling heartened by his visit to Philadelphia, he mustered the courage to visit Ripley Hitchcock, editor of one of the larger publishing houses in New York City, Appleton and Company. After looking at the newspaper articles Crane had presented, the obviously impressed Hitchcock asked if he had something they could make a book of. A few days later, Crane sent him clippings of his war story. If he hoped for a quick answer from Hitchcock, Crane was to be disappointed. After being offered a job of a traveling correspondent for Bacheller, Crane left the city without hearing a word from Hitchcock. The summer of 1894 had brought devastating droughts across the American Midwest, killing cattle and turning arable farmland to dust. Hardest hit were farms in Nebraska where people were starving and in desperate need of aid. Though many stories had already been written to date, Bacheller wanted Crane to cover it, thinking he would find an interesting angle, and produce dispatches that would be gritty, honest and thorough. As he traveled, Crane sent Hitchcock his itinerary along with the addresses of where he planned to stay just in case the editor might hear any news about *The Red Badge of Courage* from Hitchcock.

Crane arrived in Lincoln, Nebraska in late January. He interviewed both politicians and farmers, spending about six days traveling to farms in the area. Taking a train to the small town of Eddyville, he and the other passengers were stranded by a snowstorm that sent temperatures plunging well below zero. To proceed further toward Eddyville, he hired a driver and wagon but was forced to wait out the storm in a small hotel. Many trains were derailed by the storm, and families were found frozen to death in their homes. Touched by the devastation and suffering he saw, Crane wrote two sketches, "Nebraska's Bitter Fight for Life" and "Waiting for Spring."

During one leg of his Nebraska trek, Crane passed an old clapboard hotel, painted pale blue, in a small prairie town along a dirt road that at the time seemed deserted. From this solitary scene would come the setting for the story "The Blue Hotel." Back in Lincoln, at the offices of *The Nebraska State Journal*, he met young Willa Cather, two years his junior. A student at Nebraska State University, Cather, who would become a renowned novelist herself, was a correspondent for the *Journal*; she had edited some of the segments of *The Red Badge of Courage* the paper had carried, and she was anxious to meet Crane. Cather grilled him with questions about his life and his writing, but Crane remained evasive. On his last night in Lincoln, Cather returned to the newspaper office late after completing an assignment and found Crane wandering the halls alone. He was despondent, and she encouraged him to speak candidly about his troubles. She replied to his many fatalistic remarks that in ten years he would be laughing over this present bitterness, to which he retorted, "I can't wait ten years. I haven't the time." [Stallman, 132]

Other than having little money, his troubles included not having heard from Appleton and Company. Soon after, though, in early February, Hitchcock send word that Crane's novel had been accepted for publication. The conditions of the contract were terrible, but Crane was in no position to negotiate. He wrote back, agreeing to the conditions, and promised to edit the manuscript at his next stop in New Orleans. With a quick stopover in Hot Springs, Arkansas, he arrived in New Orleans in time for Mardi Gras. Reinvigorated after his bleak days in Nebraska, he was captivated by the colors, the smells, and the sounds of the city, which left him in high spirits. His buoyant mood was reflected in the glib letters he sent to his friends back in New York. His next stop was Galveston, Texas. Expecting to find there the "wild West", he was surprised to see that Galveston looked very much like New England, with prim two-story homes facing the Gulf, which might easily have been mistaken for the coast of the Atlantic. It wasn't until he reached San Antonio that Crane felt he had found the true pulse of the West. On a trip to the Alamo, he heard stories of Confederate troops, Mexican raids, longhorn cattle drives, and, of course, the famous battle that had taken place there. Towering over neighboring buildings, the Alamo was special to Crane, who found it "as eloquent as an old battle flag." [Davis, 110]

While traveling, Crane sent columns to Bacheller and wrote a number of short stories and sketches, fleshing out ideas and cataloging events of his journey in dozens more on his return to New York. He enjoyed juxtaposing the East and West, especially creating spoofs of Wild West legends and the Easterners' ideas about them. There was something about the people of the West that appealed to him—aside from their bragging and tall tales, he found them to be truer than their Eastern counterparts. Taking a train into Mexico, Crane found adventure and a place where he said he could easily lose himself. Hiring a horse and a guide, he investigated the countryside, wearing huge spurs, a sombrero, and a serape. This quest proved almost fatal when a band of drunken Mexican bandits came swooping down on the adobe roadhouse where he and his guide had bedded down for the night. The two men escaped by galloping off on their horses Wild West style, with the bandits in hot pursuit. Had they not run smack into a regiment of Mexican cavalry, the *Rurales*, the outcome might have been much different. As with all his escapades, this event would find its way into a story called "One Dash—Horses."

Throughout the duration of his extensive travels, Crane wrote regularly to Nellie Crouse—a woman who he'd met only on one previous occasion.

They had been introduced at a tea given by Lucius Button back in January. She was visiting New York from Akron, Ohio, and while Crane was immediately taken by Crouse, he didn't write her until he knew his book would be published—possibly to bolster his confidence. In letters he was less then discreet, confessing deep feelings for her even though he hardly knew her—almost as he'd done with Willa Cather. After spending a month in the Mexican wilds, he came to the city of *Puebla*, and saw a girl who reminded him of Crouse. Whether this was absolutely true or not, he wrote to her saying that the sight of the girl made him run to the railroad office crying, "What is the shortest route to New York?" [Stallman, 150] Regardless, the assignment was over and he soon returned to the city. Back on the East coast, tan and healthy, but with empty pockets, Crane regaled his friends and family with stories of his excursion through the mid-West to Mexico, laced with his limited knowledge of Spanish.

The Lover and the Tale

While he was away, several of Crane's literary friends founded the Lantern Club, originally the "Lanthorn Club." In an added story on the roof of an old building, in a section of New York known as *Monkey Hill*, they set up headquarters. Considering themselves to be literary lights, they used a ship's lantern as their symbol. Here Crane could get at least one good meal a day. For the most part, Crane hung out at the apartments of his friends, living mostly on coffee and cigars. Although his friends urged him to cut back on caffeine and tobacco, and insisted he see a dentist (his teeth were in terrible shape), for the most part their pleas went unheeded. Upon leaving the city to spend the summer at his brother Edmund's house, Crane gave his editors the address of the *Lantern Club* as his place of residence. If Crane could have had his way, he would never write in the summer—which he considered camping season—but he needed the money. He'd begun a new novel, *George's Mother*, which was intended as a sequel to *Maggie*. The character, George, an exaggerated version of Crane, is the most autobiographical of all his works. While spending time at the Twin Lakes campsite, he wrote to Hitchcock to send the galley proofs of *The Red Badge of Courage* so he could work on then there. In letters to friends back in New York, he said to some that he was writing a great deal while on vacation in the country, to others he confessed not to have written much at all. Bicycles had become the rage, and in a letter to his friend Hawkins, he compared bicycles to horses, giving the latter the greater preference. "Your can push your lifeless old bicycles around the country, but a slim-limbed thoroughbred's dauntless spirit is better."

[Stallman, 154] His brother Edmund recalled that Crane's health never failed to thrive after a few hours on horseback in the mountains outside Hartwood.

Reviews on his book of poetry, *The Black Riders*, trickled in throughout out the summer. Some were favorable, and some were severe. The imagery used in his verses gave critics many opportunities to elaborate on their displeasure with what were often brutal parodies. While many praised his courage and originality, others claimed that what he wrote wasn't poetry at all. Reviews from Britain were more favorable than those in the United States; nonetheless, Crane stood by the work, often stating that *The Black Riders* was by far his favorite of all of his writings. His reason was that the composition of a book of poetry, more so than a book fiction, required prodigious effort. As a result of his newly acquired fame, he received fan mail even at Hartwood. He claimed that if he answered all the letters he'd received he would oblige the Hartwood post office to expand its operation.

The Red Badge of Courage made its formal appearance on September 27, 1894; sales took off quickly, and the book appeared on bestseller lists around the country. Appleton and Company sold the book in England, as well, settling for a flat fee with no royalties. Unaware of this decision, Crane—who chose to remain in the dark about contracts and negotiations—received very little from British sales. Unlike *Black Riders*, the war novel brought mostly rave reviews for its vigorous authenticity. The Detroit Free Press said the book "will give you so vivid a picture of the emotions and the horrors of the battlefield that you will pray your eyes may never look upon the reality." [Davis, 127] Crane's friend and mentor William Dean Howells was not quite so kind, saying the book's strength lay in the fact that it offered promise of better things to come. Crane never made public mention of his reaction to Howells's review, which appeared in *Harper's Bazaar*—possibly because of the implied faith in Crane's promise as a writer.

Crane now had money in his pockets, and he began making grand plans to spend it. After purchasing needed clothing, he spent a goodly sum on an elaborate Mexican saddle and bridle. Still, by mid-October his discomfort with his growing fame began to surface. He moved all his belongings from New York to Edmund's house in Hartwood, as if to distance himself from the trappings of success. From Hartwood, he subscribed to a clipping bureau based in Boston. Upon receiving the reviews, he was pleased to see that, out of forty-one, only six were negative. However, it angered him that he found less favor in New York than in any other city. *Red Badge* entered its fourth edition, and argument began over who had discovered this rising talent. With a flash of dry wit, Crane said he was glad to be discovered but "thought it probable only one Columbus could have discovered me." [Sufrin, 87] He started a new novel, which gave Crane reason to doubt his abilities, as letters to his publisher Hitchcock indicate hesitancy and vacillation over the manuscript of what would become *The Third Violet*. This book, a romance, was an about-face for him, not only in subject matter but also in style, and Crane knew the writing was weaker than that of his other work and somewhat out of character for him.

The Philistine Society, a group of newspapermen from Buffalo, New York, invited Crane to a dinner they were to hold in his honor. Previously, he'd written a piece for their magazine, *The Philistine*, but he was surprised that they wanted to honor him. He borrowed clothes from his friends in order to look the part of the successful writer, but as it turned out the event was a roast at Crane's expense, which angered some of the guests. Crane, however, enjoyed every minute. When one guest rose to leave in disgust, Crane's friend Hawkins stopped him saying that Crane much preferred this lighthearted touch to a solemn eulogy, and the man sat back down. Hawkins was right, for Crane never felt he'd been offended and even boasted of the event in a letter to Nellie Crouse. As the result of the roast, he went on to become a close friend of Elbert Hubbard, the man who had organized the event.

By January, Crane was in demand everywhere, and even family members clamored to see him. It pained him that he wasn't able answer the demands of his friends to see him. Ultimately, though, Crane's biggest fear with success was that he might become complacent in his work, thereby stunting his literary growth. Editors begged him for more war stories, assuming that he could write others. At first he complied, visiting Civil War battlefields and writing five Civil War stories in the space of a year. Finally, though, he decided to stop. Writing to Nellie Crouse, he complained, "Hang all war stories." In the short story "The Veteran," he recycles the Henry Fleming from *The Red Badge of Courage* and kills him off in the end. Flush with the success of *The Red Badge of Courage*, Appleton and Company agreed to release a newly edited version of *Maggie*, which pleased Crane a great deal. S.S. McClure, who wanted to cash in on Crane's reputation, challenged him to write a novel about politics and sent him to Washington D.C. on assignment. Overall, his junket to the capitol was a failure, as Crane's interest in politics was scant to begin with and diminished in the course of interviews he had with politicians. Crane said on his return that politicians were so duplicitous that "it would take a double-barreled shotgun to disclose their inward feelings." [Sufrin, 87]

In the early months of 1896, Crane's letters to Nellie Crouse grew longer and more serious in tone. He suggested that she come east and inquired whether he should go to Akron. He also revealed to her his deep-seated despondency, which may have been alarming to her, for the two were never again to meet in person, and eventually, by March, the flow of letters ended. It is uncertain who was the last to write or quite how the end came. In the meantime, he stayed close to the home of his brother Edmund, having purchased a horse that he'd fallen in love with and named Peanuts. Crane and his brother had great fun in racing their horses around the windy roads of Hartwood. Edmund's daughter Edith recalled that the horse was extremely unpredictable and knew how to unlatch the door of its stall—and that her Uncle Crane nicknamed the horse Monkeyshines and loved it dearly.

Restless about his future, Crane returned to New York in April; he immediately invited his friends to his new apartment West 23rd Street for poker. This was a short-lived experiment at normalcy, for soon after he took a flat in an apartment house frequented by prostitutes.

George's Mother was released early in 1896 to mixed reviews. William Dean Howells praised the work, feeling that both *Maggie* and *George's Mother* far surpassed *The Red Badge of Courage* in quality and style. Crane took the liberty of sending a copy of *George's Mother* to New York's Commissioner of Police, Theodore Roosevelt. Roosevelt wrote back to Crane to thank him, saying that *The Red Badge of Courage* remained his favorite. Roosevelt covered the Lower West Side, and to stay on top of his officers' conduct he walked the streets in disguise late at night. The *New York Journal* offered Crane an assignment to report on the "Tenderloin District" of San Francisco—a West Coast version of the Bowery. The name of this part of the city originated from a police captain, accused of graft, who said after he was put in command of the district that he had "[been eating] chuck for a long time, and now [he would help himself to] some of the tenderloin." [Sufrin, 89]

When he returned to New York, Crane resumed his former tactics to ferret out stories as he'd done when he lived in the Bowery. He spent much of his time in police courts, opium dens, beer parlors, and the other all-night dives of the locals. On the evening of September 15, Crane made an appointment to meet several chorus girls at the Turkish Smoking Parlors on West 29th Street for an interview. After speaking with them at Broadway Gardens, he escorted one of the women to the cable car, leaving the others behind. When he returned, he saw that they were being arrested by the police for soliciting, and he rushed back to assist the women, who by now were hysterical. One cried out that Crane was her husband, and he agreed, so she was released. The other woman, Dora Clark, was carted off to the police station, where she spent the night in jail. Crane let it be known that he would show up the next morning to testify on Dora Clark's behalf.

Crane shot a telegram to Roosevelt saying he was going to press charges against the policeman, Charles Becker. Roosevelt ignored the telegram and stuck by his police officer's story that Dora Clark was guilty. In spite of being advised by many of his friends to let the matter drop, Crane was now compelled by what he considered a true cause. The newspapers had a field day with the story, defaming the up-and-coming author with glaring headlines. At first as he was portrayed as a knight in shining armor ready to rescue the damsel in distress; later the coverage became ugly. When Crane was called to testify in court, under heavy cross-examination his own character came into question. He was accused of being addicted to opium and of living with various girls in his apartment; the prosecuting attorney used everything at his disposal to discredit Crane's testimony. Brought into the case as proof of the allegations against him was the fact that had lied about being the husband of one of the girls. The prosecutor's main point became: If he'd lied once, why wouldn't he lie again?

Some newspaper reports cried out against the distortion of Crane's private affairs, saying the police intimidation against the author was an outrage. Others sided with the police, calling Crane a liar. He stood firm against the abuse to his character, but the publicity did more harm than good when it came to credibility and his career. A principle was at stake, though, as he told the press: "It may be against my interest to act as I did, but by Heaven I'd do it every time, though I have some little reputation which I have starved myself to acquire, and though I should lose it by my action." [Stallman, 231] Sadly, Crane did not live to see the outcome of this case. In 1913, Becker was found guilty of having underworld connections; he was convicted of murder and sentenced to death, becoming the first New York City policeman to be put to death in the electric chair. Many of Crane's close friends stood by him, but the literary elite, whose favor he was just starting to win, left him. Garland advised him to go back to Hartwood and write another book, and that was what he was ready to do. An assignment from Bacheller-Johnson to cover the turmoil that was just beginning in Cuba provided Crane with a ticket out of town.

ACTIVE SERVICE

On November 14, 1896, Crane arrived by train in Jacksonville, Florida. Fearful that bad press had preceded him, he registered at the St. James Hotel under the pseudonym of Samuel Carleton. In the previous decade, Jacksonville had become a busy tourist seaport, offering the allure of tropical weather and an exotic landscape. Irving Bacheller had sent Crane to the city as a starting point for coverage of the ongoing Cuban revolt. This prosperous city served as the headquarters of the Cuban Junta heading up plans to overthrow Spanish rule. Because of the possibility of a full-scale war, reporters, mercenaries, adventurers, and opportunists poured into the city, hoping to catch a ship to either see or become involved in the action. Stephen quickly learned that it was no easy task to gain passage to the island because of neutrality and navigation laws. There was nothing to do but wait, so he spent much of his time in dimly lit bars and brothels.

One such haunt was Hotel de Dream, where Stephen was introduced to the hostess, Cora (Stewart) Taylor. Taylor rented the house from Ethel Dreme, whose name had inspired that of the hotel. The hotel was described as a fine "nightclub"—a term that at the time implied a house of prostitution. However, the Hotel de Dream was considered superior to other such establishments because its guests were required to uphold a certain standard of behavior, which originated with Taylor herself. Born Cora Howorth, Taylor had been raised in Boston, the daughter of affluent and cultured parents. Her grandfather had owned an art gallery and her father, John Howorth, had been a painter. Her second marriage had been to Captain Donald William Stewart, the son of an English baronet. Although this marriage was in difficulty, Captain Stewart refused to grant her a divorce. In order to build a new life for herself in Jacksonville, Cora had adopted the surname Taylor. Six years older than Crane, she was well-read, intelligent, and extremely independent. She ran the Hotel de Dream as if it were a parlor and not a bordello, forbidding the consumption of hard liquor, and required all her "girls" live elsewhere.

Crane was introduced to Taylor as Samuel Carleton, but when she learned his true identity, having read his books, she was smitten. A reporter friend of Crane's who was there on that evening said, "The news pierced the lady's very liver" and that if she "had any false notes I was then all too unskilled in recognizing authentic 'class,' or lack of it, to detect any." [Davis, 177; Stallman, 140–141] Crane had just left a girl behind in New York named Amy Leslie, who, like Taylor, was both older than Crane and fiercely independent—but in Leslie's case sixteen years older. A well-known drama critic for the *Chicago Daily News*, Leslie had at one time been an actress, replacing her given name, Lily West, with Amy Leslie for the stage.

Leslie's name had appeared on the guest list for the Philistine Society dinner, but she did not attend on the night of Crane's roast. It is unclear whether she and Crane met before or after this occasion; it is certain, however, that they spent much time together in New York during the summer of 1896. Leslie was with Crane on the Florida train, but they parted in Washington, D.C. As she was getting off the train, it was noted that she was in an emotional state, which visibly upset Crane, at least temporarily. His letters from Florida to her reveal that he planned for their time apart to be short, asking that she wait for him. After he met Taylor, though, Crane's correspondence with Leslie became sporadic. On December 15, he wrote to say he was certain to depart soon and told her that he loved her, and her alone. With the letter, he enclosed a photo of himself on horseback, looking dashing in his correspondent's garb. He did not write to her again before his departure with the *Commodore*.

To while away the hours until his departure, Crane spent a good deal of time in the company of Taylor at the Hotel de Dream. Inside the cover of a signed copy of *George's Mother* Crane gave to her, he inscribed the dedication "To an unnamed sweetheart." [Stallman, 239] Knowing the dangers he might face on this assignment, Crane made out a will, which he sent to his brother William, appointing William sole executor. One third of his estate was to go to William, another third was to go to Edmund, and the balance was to be divided between George and Townley. The will was detailed enough to include the horse Peanuts, as well as his short stories, unfinished novels, and manuscripts. In the same letter, he stood by his decision to defend Dora Clark: ". . . I see no reason why, if I should live a thousand years, I should be ever be ashamed or humiliated by my course in the matter." [Davis, 171] With that out of the way, he was fully prepared to meet whatever the future offered him as he boarded the *Commodore* on December 31, 1896.

The wreck of the tug was a boon for Crane as a writer, in spite of the fact that he almost lost his life. The experience provided the fodder for one of his greatest literary accomplishments. Not incidentally, too, there were glorious headlines that proclaimed him a hero. Before news of the rescue arrived, some papers had reported Crane's death, increasing the dramatic tension of his eventual survival. In light of the Dora Clark affair, it was good to have the press back in his corner. One New York paper offered him a large sum of money for a scoop on the disaster. Crane turned it down, honoring his commitment to his present employer. In a wire to Bacheller dated January 4, he said he needed time to recuperate before he could write about the sinking of the tug. Within a few days he wrote a dispatch that closely followed the facts, but he knew there would be more to write.

In the days immediately following his rescue, Crane began writing "The Open Boat" at the Hotel de Dream, but he had trouble making any real progress. Part of the problem was that Taylor hovered over him constantly. Feeling stifled by her attention, on January 7 he renewed his search for a vessel to Cuba, for he realized that he would have to escape the distractions in town if he was going to finish the story. Completed during a short trip he took to New York, this 9,000-word story would later become one of Crane's best-known pieces. Told from multiple points of view, "The Open Boat" explores the psychic climate of a group of men struggling to survive in a dinghy at sea. Delving into how the actions of each individual character determines the collective fate of all, and exploring the events that have led their lives to become inextricably intertwined, the story creates a literary tapestry that is both vivid and horrifying. The work, too, is largely biographical.

On his return to Jacksonville, he continued to look for passage to Cuba. By March 11, however, he became convinced his efforts would be fruitless. The revenue cutters were now rigidly enforcing the neutrality laws, and few ships were getting through. Crane decided to investigate the Greco-Turkish War that was unfolding in Europe. In a letter to his brother William, he wrote:

> I have been for over a month among the swamps further South wading miserably to and fro in an attempt to avoid our derned U.S. Navy. And it can't be done. I am through trying. I have changed all my plans and am going to Crete. I expect to sail from NY one week from next Saturday. Expect me in P.J. [Port Jervis] on Thursday. Give my love to all and assure them of my remembrances." [Stallman, 260]

For reasons unknown, Crane never made it to Port Jervis. William hurried to New York to spend a short time with his brother before he set sail for Europe; this would be the last time William would see Crane alive. Linson remembered encountering a transformed Stephen Crane during this time, sporting a suit that fit, combed hair, and a trimmed moustache. Heading to his favorite spot in Linson's studio apartment, he said that Crane sat on the couch, rather than sprawling his length across it as was his habit. Because Linson had been to Greece, Crane barraged him with questions about the country and its inhabitants. Over dinner, Crane mentioned that there was a special woman in his life whom he hated to leave behind. Asking Linson what he should do, the artist told him if he loved her he should marry her. Characteristically, Crane never mentioned Taylor's name.

Crane didn't need worry about leaving Taylor behind, though, for she had already decided to follow him to Greece. She settled her affairs, and purchased a steamer ticket to England. In addition to leaving Jacksonville post-haste, she had made up her mind to become the world's first female war correspondent. Accompanied by her friend Charlotte Ruedy, Taylor traveled on the same ship as did Crane; she wasn't introduced to Crane's friends or family at the ship's dock, and during the crossing they remained apart.

Arriving in England, Crane was met with instant celebrity. His modesty and reticence impressed the British as atypical in an American. He made contact with his European publisher, William Heinemann, who had made

Crane's books bestsellers in England. At a lunch held in his honor at the Savoy Club, Crane was introduced to such literary figures as Anthony Hope, Justin H. McCarthy, Sir James Barrie, and Harold Frederic. Richard Harding Davis, an American correspondent for the *London Times* set to leave for Greece himself, hosted the luncheon. Davis and Crane had been compared by critics, and this critical history hindered any deep friendship between the two. They did, however, wind up sharing a train to Paris on the first leg of their journey to Greece. Transferring to a French steamer at Marseilles, they arrived in Athens, where the sight of the warships in the harbor impressed Crane more than had the city's famous ruins. Taylor traveled concurrently, dispatching her stories under the pseudonym Imogene Carter. Traveling mostly on her own, she wound up at the Greek headquarters in Pharsala hoping to get an interview with Crown Prince Constantine. However, when she arrived, the prince was ordering a retreat from the city, as the Turks were swiftly closing in. Just when it seemed that Crane would get the armed conflict he had waited months to witness in Cuba, he contracted dysentery.

After some time, fellow correspondents grew disgruntled with Crane and his female companion. Davis commented that Crane seemed to be "a genius with no responsibilities of any sort to anyone." [Sufrin, 105] Thinking that Crane had a toothache rather than dysentery, Davis wrote in a letter that Crane had been at the front a mere fifteen minutes before composing a 1300-word story on his turn in the vicinity of the conflict. Davis went on to say that if it hadn't been for the woman Crane would have been at the front, toothache or not. At the battle of Velestino, however, reporters remembered Crane as indifferent to the bullets, sitting on an ammunition box smoking a cigarette while others stayed in the trenches. The correspondents, with Taylor among them, were some of the last spectators to leave the front before the Turks broke through the battle lines. On their way down the mountain, Crane rescued a puppy, which he named "Velestino, the Journal dog." By the time the war was over, Crane had written of so many retreats on the Greek side that he had begun to wonder whether there would be victories to report. None would come, for an armistice was signed on May 20 and quickly put an end to what turned out to be a thirty-day war.

AN UPTURNED FACE

While he was in Greece, Crane corresponded with his friend Hawkins concerning a sum of money that he owed to Amy Leslie. During their last encounter, she'd given Crane $800 to set up in an account for her. Always careless with money, Crane had put the money into his own account instead and finally spent it. When she sent him a letter asking for it, he replied that didn't have it. Now in an attempt to pay her back, he used Hawkins as his go-between in the States to send her installments as he could afford them—an arrangement that Hawkins, understandably, came to resent. In his letters, Crane would tell Hawkins to send Leslie his love, even as all of his affections for the present were focused on Taylor.

In June, the couple returned to England, and as Taylor's husband still refused to grant her a divorce they chose not to return immediately to America. Installed in the British literary community, Crane made friends with many writers, and he found these critics a good deal kinder than those back in the States. Ford Madox Ford admitted that he disliked Crane upon their first meeting, but he later came to admire him, referring to him as "an Apollo with starry eyes. . . . There are few men I have liked—nay, indeed, revered . . . more than Crane. He was so frail and so courageous, so preyed upon and so generous, so weighted down by misfortunes and so erect in his carriage. And he was such a beautiful genius." [Sufrin, 111–112] The literati were receptive to Taylor as well, even when it was known she was "a woman with a past." Not uncharacteristically, Crane's letters home make no mention of her at all. In fact, letters to William seem to suggest that eventually he would come home and settle down in Port Jervis.

The couple moved into a large house called Ravensbrook, adding to the household a servant, the rescued puppy, and Charlotte Ruedy, who remained with them for a time. Located twenty miles south of London, Ravensbrook is situated in an area known as Limpsfield-Oxted. Here Crane and Taylor began a pattern of extravagance that would eventually cause them much travail. The expansive house, full of empty rooms, needed furniture, so food, supplies, and furniture were purchased on credit. As they developed a reputation for lavish dinner parties and word spread of Crane's hospitality, guests descended upon Ravensbrook, many uninvited. As Taylor spent money the couple did not have, Crane wrote checks with a new fury to pay the accumulating bills. His new agent in America, Paul Revere Reynolds, received many pleas for money, often for advances for pieces that Crane had not yet written. Reynolds had an agreement with Crane which gave him a flat ten percent of everything he sold, and he was given free reign to sell everything Crane wrote, wherever he could have it published. In England, his agent was James B. Pinker, whom Crane also repeatedly asked for advances.

The Third Violet had been released, and it was a book that even Crane had no faith in. On the flyleaf of a copy sent to a friend he wrote, "This book is even worse than any of the others." [Stallman, 296] Fans who admired *The Red Badge of Courage* were disappointed. One magazine admitted the book was reviewed solely because of the fame of the author; otherwise, it would have been ignored. But he remained impervious, and 1897 would prove to be one of Crane's most prolific years. With thoughts turned homeward, he wrote on the trip he made out West, culminating in the stories "The Blue Hotel" and "The Bride Comes to Yellow Sky." In August, he and Taylor visited friends in Ireland, the Frederics. On the way, they were involved in a carriage accident, after which the Frederics insisted the couple remain with them to recuperate. The visit lasted three weeks, during which time Crane wrote his observations about life in Ireland.

Back in England, Crane had the opportunity to meet the Polish author Joseph Conrad, whose *The Nigger of the Narcissus* he had recently read. Introduced by Sidney Pawling, an editor from Heinemann, at a luncheon in London, the two writers became fast friends, in spite of their fourteen-year difference in age. Conrad would say about this meeting that although he was the elder he felt Crane his senior in writing talent and ability. The luncheon spanned the afternoon, and after it Pawling left the writers to talk until late in the night. In the November after their initial meeting, Crane journeyed to Essex to visit the Conrads. At the time, Conrad's wife, Jessie, was pregnant and could not travel. In February, though, after the birth of their son, Borys, the Conrads arrived at Ravensbrook for a stay of ten days. The two families got along famously, with Crane and Taylor constantly fussing over little Borys. Later, Conrad wrote to tell Crane how much he missed him and even suggested that the two families take a house together for several months; but this was not to be.

In the last months of 1897, Crane found himself sinking deeper and deeper into debt, struggling frantically to keep up with the demands of his creditors. At the moment when things seemed to be at their worst, Amy Leslie decided to sue Crane for the remaining money he owed her—over $500, the equivalent of approximately $9,000 in 2001. The story found its way into the headlines of several prominent American newspapers. The *Chicago Evening Post* noted that Crane was hiding out in London, and warned him that if he still had a "red badge of courage," he would "have plenty of opportunity to exhibit it." [Davis, 238] Older brother William came to the rescue, and was able to settle the matter out of court. No evidence remains of who paid the settlement, nor the amount.

On February 15, 1898, word came that the U.S. battleship *Maine* had been fired upon and sunk in Havana harbor, killing 266 men. War with Spain was now imminent. President McKinley, however, proceeded with caution, requesting a full inquiry. By March the findings absolved the U.S. Navy of any blame, and while Spain was not mentioned, no one doubted its guilt in the matter. By April, Crane was convinced that he must get back to America and enlist in the Navy. While he and Cora had talked about finding cheaper lodgings, now there was no time, for he was in a rush to join the war. Crane and Conrad scurried through London trying to raise money for a steamer ticket. They ended up at *Blackwood's Magazine*, where Crane was paid an advance on articles to be cabled to them from the front. Conrad recalled that Crane's "white-faced excitement frightened [him]." He added, "Nothing could have held him back. He was ready to swim the ocean . . . ." [Stallman, 347] Crane found passage on board the *Germanic*, steaming out of Liverpool on April 13. Crane probably knew he was physically unfit for acceptance into the Navy, but he was willing to risk everything for the chance. Word came when he reached New York that the *New York World* wanted to hire him as one of its correspondents. Once that was settled, he wasted no time in leaving for Key West, Florida, which was already swarming with reporters. When he arrived at Key West, he was by greeted Sylvester Scovel, a friend from his time in Greece, under whom he now would work. Scovel had already gained notoriety for reporting from behind the scenes in Cuba, and Scovel's acquaintance with many influential military officers enabled him to help Crane to gain access to some of the strategic hot spots of the war.

Americans had a voracious appetite for breaking news and blow-by-blow reporting. Bigger news organizations like the *New York World*, Randolph Hearst's *Journal*, and the Associated Press spent vast sums of money to rent dispatch boats in order to keep their reporters in the midst of the action. Likewise, thousands of dollars were spent on telegraph cables for dispatches that ticked between Florida and New York. It was during this time that new precedents in reporting were being set, as news stories were expected to be produced whether or not there was any news available. Managing editors demanded hair-raising stories, the "inside scoop" on particular battles, and human-interest stories of heroic exploits, all meant to "keep the presses rolling" and the public digging for pocket change. In essence, then, what might begin as a skirmish in Florida was turned into a siege on the front page by the time the item reached New York. Crane traveled with Scovel on the tug *Three Friends* and the two spent most of their time aboard in their bunks because the rolling pitch of the sea made it impossible to write in any other fashion. The dispatch boats were always in danger as they flitted among the big warships. One boat was mistaken for a Spanish gunboat and chased down by an American cruiser. In Key West between battles, Crane drank, played poker, and worked on his own writing, for by now he had tired of straight reporting.

In June, he was witness to a series of land battles in Cuba. While on the island Crane had contracted malaria, but never it let his slacken his pace. For he sought out the most grueling and dangerous of missions, and began to cover the activities of Theodore Roosevelt's Rough Riders. While Roosevelt was too busy to acknowledge Crane, he still admired that Roosevelt was able to set aside his political ambitions to fight in the war. During the battle at San Juan Hill, Crane and another correspondent found Edward Marshall from the *Journal* shot through the spine and lying in a field. They took Marshall to a dressing station, after which Crane trekked several miles through the jungle to find Marshall's dispatch. In another battle, under fire, Crane carried water to soldiers sweltering in the 108° heat behind the enemy lines. A correspondent for London's *Daily Chronicle* wrote that Crane looked, by all appearances, to be the last one expected to become a hero, yet manifested "the highest and truest courage." [Stallman, 371]

By July, the war was over and Crane was very ill. Aboard the *City of Washington*, bound for Virginia, he was ordered by the doctor to stay apart from the wounded and injured soldiers. Dressed in the same clothes he'd worn for more than three weeks, he slept on the deck. While recuperating in New York, Crane traveled to Saranac Lake to see a specialist about his health, suspecting that he had tuberculosis. The doctor there, however, gave the prognosis that he was not seriously ill.

There is no indication that he contacted Taylor, who was waiting for his return to England. Rather, he went back to Cuba, anonymously taking up residence in Havana. Deeply in debt and with very little income, he began to write as he had done in the past: in order to eat. Why he went into hiding without contacting Taylor is unclear. Some have speculated that he was running from gambling debts or suffering from depression related to his illness.

Frantic, Taylor tried every means possible to learn of Crane's fate, and she was deeply hurt when she found out from the British consul that he was still alive. Due to her intercession, Crane's British publisher wired him $250, a sum that would return him safely to England. Stopping in New York City, Crane tried his best to persuade Taylor to meet him in the States, but this was to no avail. He called their interaction a "duel at long range, with ink." [Stallman, 441] Soon after, he booked passage on a steamer bound for England.

In Mammoth they moved into a 14th-century estate called Brede Manor—a damp, drafty house not conducive to recovery from tuberculosis and the lasting effects of malaria. Immediately upon his return, Crane was inundated with the demands of creditors, and while the pair had planned to live frugally it was never within their grasp to do so. They hired a staff for the house and began repairs and the planting of an expansive rose garden. Meanwhile, Taylor expected Crane to write enough to solve the problem of funding. He did as she expected, sitting in his "porch room" day after day writing, but the work he produced in this period never achieved the quality of his earlier publications. While flooding his agent, Pinker, with light, clever stories, he demanded and begged for advances and immediate payments, as though Pinker were himself a publisher. Paul Reynolds had dropped Crane because of the continual demands for money. In September of 1899, Crane asked Pinker to secure for him an assignment in South Africa covering the Boer War, but this would never materialize.

To celebrate the new century, Taylor planned a Christmas and New Year's party lasting a full week. While Brede Manor was filled with dancing and singing, Crane was unusually quiet and reserved. Later that night, he suffered a severe hemorrhage, and one of the guests rode a bicycle through the snow to fetch a doctor. He had improved sufficiently by mid-January to return to his writing. However much he wrote and sold, though, what money he made was not nearly enough to cover the expenses of the large house and the couple's entertainments. In April he suffered another hemorrhage, after which the doctor suggested a dryer climate. Crane made out a will leaving to Taylor all his personal belongings—but after his death his brother William would not honor this aspect of the will. In one of his last letters, Crane wrote to a friend on behalf of Joseph Conrad, who was also nearly destitute, to inquire if he could help him find a position in civil service.

As Crane's health deteriorated, Taylor made plans to take him to a famous treatment center for tuberculosis patients in Badenweiler, Germany. She solicited everyone she could think of to help finance the expensive trip, which required special air-beds and an invalid carriage. She sent a cable to John Hay at the War Department in Washington for a contribution to the saving of Crane's life. In the end, she received contributions from J.P. Morgan, Andrew Carnegie, Joseph Pulitzer, and Lady Randolph Churchill. Joseph Conrad remained convinced that Crane would prefer to die at his own home, but Taylor was too strong-willed to be swayed and Crane too weak to protest. They arrived at Badenweiler on May 28, but by then the doctors could do nothing. For a week Crane suffered with a high fever, and his bed sheets had to be changed several times each day. He died before sunrise on June 5. His body was returned to the United States, where a funeral was held in New York at the Metropolitan Temple, conducted by a Methodist minister who had been a lifelong friend of the Crane family. Stephen Crane was buried in the family plot in Elizabeth, New Jersey.

Before returning to England, Taylor met with Crane's family, and his brother Edmund gave to her Crane's scrapbook filled with the clippings of his reviews and newspaper articles. For a time Cora attempted to make a living writing, finishing some of Crane's stories and writing a few of her own. She thought to write his biography but found the task was beyond her abilities. Within two years, she returned to Florida and opened a new house, similar to Hotel de Dream, called the Court. After Captain Stewart died, she married a man many years younger than she. She was divorced a short time later, in 1909. In 1910, Taylor died and was buried in Jacksonville, and the name "Cora E. Crane" was inscribed on her tombstone.

Immediately following his death, it seemed Crane's work would be obscured by the new century. H.G. Wells wrote in 1915, "America can produce such a supreme writer as Stephen Crane—the best writer of English in the last half-century. . . . But America won't own such children . . . she'll never know she had a Stephen Crane." [Sufrin, 153] Yet, with a biography written by Thomas Beer in the 1920s, there was a resurgence of interest in Crane and his works—an interest that has continued to the present. And because much of Crane's literary out put has been adopted into the canon of Western literature, studied in universities, and explored in scholarly publications, the staying power of such stories as *The Red Badge of Courage* and *Maggie* speaks to not only the historical relevance of this work, but also the insight with which Crane was able to depict the struggles inherent in the human condition.

Works Cited

Davis, Linda H. *Badge of Courage: The Life of Stephen Crane*. Boston: Houghton Mifflin, 1998.

Stallman, Robert W. *Stephen Crane: A Biography*. New York: George Braziller, 1968.

Sufrin, Mark. *Stephen Crane*. New York: Atheneum, 1992.

The Vanishing Acts of Stephen Crane

Upon learning of the death of Stephen Crane, Henry James wrote, "What a brutal, needless extinction—what an unmitigated unredeemed catastrophe! I think of him with such a sense of possibilities and powers!"[1] The tenor of James's lament was virtually unanimous among turn-of-the-century literati: Crane's talent had been prodigious, almost shockingly so, and the promise of his life had been extinguished much too soon. William Dean Howells declared him to have been the most "distinctive and vital talent" ever produced in America;[2] Joseph Conrad, who openly envied that talent during his friend's life, reflected in later years that "as an artist he [was] non-comparable . . . though it was his fate . . . to fall early in the fray."[3]

Stephen Crane had burst from the ranks of New York newspaper writers in 1893 with his tragic novella of Bowery life, *Maggie: A Girl of the Streets*—the story of a young girl who, after descending through a tenement-world of shattered illusions and into a life of prostitution, commits suicide. His literary fame was assured a year later with *The Red Badge of Courage*, his novel of the Civil War, which, as Joseph Conrad later recalled, "detonated . . . on our literary sensibilities with the impact and force of a twelve-inch shell charged with a very high explosive."[4] That Crane should have been capable of writing such a book at the age of 21 seemed to many nothing short of miraculous; *Red Badge* is a masterpiece of war literature, remarkable for its harrowing and realistic depiction of battle in the mind of a young soldier, but for Crane, who had never experienced war, it was purely an act of imagination. However brilliant these and other works were, Crane never had a chance to outlive his status as the *enfant terrible* of American literature. He died of tuberculosis in June of 1900, at the age of 28.

If there was general agreement about the significance of Crane's contribution at the time of his death, though, there has seldom been much consensus in the critical evaluation of his *oeuvre* in the century since. In the last seven years of his life, Crane produced a wide-ranging body of work—novels, short stories, poems, travelogues, and hard-boiled journalistic sketches—and critics have rarely, if ever, agreed on what to think of his work as a whole. There has been no shortage of labels: realist, naturalist, impressionist, symbolist, modernist.[5] Each of these descriptors may apply intermittently, but none fully captures his elusive aesthetic sensibility. As Crane himself wrote to editor Ripley Hitchcock in 1896, "I cannot help vanishing and disappearing and dissolving. It is my foremost trait."[6]

The whole of Crane's career, with its startling rise and sudden end, was contained in the tumultuous 1890s. Henry Adams, one of the ablest chroniclers of his or any age, remarks that "during this last decade every one talked, and seemed to feel *fin-de-siècle*" [7]—and, indeed, the turbulent changes then taking place in America seemed to announce the end of one era and the inception of another. As the movement of western expansion and the forces of industrialism were re-mapping America's rural landscape, innovations in the technology of manufacture transformed the character of labor in urban centers, which were teeming with immigrants. The adoption of the international gold standard in 1893 seemed to augur a new age of global capitalism, even as the country sank into economic depression. In the works of realist writers like William Dean Howells—an important mentor figure for Crane—fortunes are made and lost; and the ambitions of an ill-served underclass are thwarted in a time of growing social turmoil. Dreams of advancement assumed for many a grand shape, but hard new social and economic realities announced that old models of progress rested on romantic illusions that were inadequate to describe the relationships of the individual to an increasingly complex world. At the 1893 World's Columbian Exposition in Chicago, the admiring eyes of record crowds absorbed the promise of new inventions and products alongside bold proclamations for an ever-richer American tomorrow; it was here that Americans rode the first Ferris wheel and had their first taste of hamburgers, Cracker Jack, diet sodas, and Juicy Fruit chewing gum, beneath the grand facades that were to be the architecture of American destiny. It was here, too, that Frederick Jackson Turner famously declared the age of America's restive inventiveness and rugged individualism to have closed along with the physical frontier that had inspired it. As Henry Adams writes, "Chicago asked in 1893 for the first time the question whether the American people knew where they were driving."[8]

Crane, like Adams, did not claim to know where the world was headed in 1893—Crane believed all grand theories to be "fatal" to art and literature—but he sensed the volatile work of large and indifferent historical forces that isolated individuals in ways they could scarcely comprehend, let alone master. In many of Crane's early stories of life on the Bowery in New York City—such as *Maggie: A Girl of the Streets* (1892), "A Dark-Brown Dog" (1893–4; published posthumously), or "An Experiment in Misery" (1894)—the forces that overwhelm individuals often appear to be derivatives of the social mechanisms that perpetuate the poverty and squalor of street life. Like Jacob Riis, whose 1890 exposé, *How the Other Half Lives*, revealed to many the hard realities of the urban poor, Crane brought his artistic lens to bear on conditions of extreme privation. Crane had been drawn to such scenes since he was a teenager, having developed the spine and hard-nosed instinct for depicting life on the streets as a roving newspaper reporter while still in college. In the Bowery tales, cruelty is rampant and loyalties are scarce; actions are sudden, frequently violent, and carry terrible consequences. The often unnamed characters of these stories act with a kind of reckless desperation, borne of the dawning realization that the promise of life beyond the slums will always elude them. Thus the "sudden awe" of Willie at the conclusion of "An Experiment in Misery" at the rise of the buildings surrounding him in his isolation on a park bench:

> And in the background a multitude of buildings, of pitiless hues and sternly high, were to him emblematic of a nation forcing its regal head into the clouds, throwing no downward glances; in the sublimity of its aspirations ignoring the wretches who may flounder at its feet. The roar of the city in his ear was to him the confusion of strange tongues, babbling heedlessly; it was the clink of coin, the voice of the city's hopes which were to him no hopes.[9]

Here, Willie's internal psychological anguish becomes externalized onto the landscape. This is one of Crane's signature techniques, a way of particularizing experience by presenting it through the eyes of an individual. The effect is that of a magnification, in which we discover the *terra incognita* of an individual mind by experiencing its impressions, textures, and projections first hand. In turn, this internal perspective transforms the aspect of external reality, and we are made to bear witness to a world that seems at once more distant and foreboding. This effect is brilliantly achieved in one of the more famous passages from *Maggie*, in which Maggie, her reputation and will permanently broken, is making her final march toward an off-stage suicide: "She went into the blackness of the final block. The shutters of the tall buildings were closed like grim lips. The structures seemed to have eyes that looked over her, beyond her, at other things. Afar off the lights of the avenues glittered as if from an impossible distance."[10] Vanishing into the darkness, the textual presence of Maggie is subsumed into the pitiless aspect of a city block that now seems threatening and alive.

In this we arrive at one of Crane's central ironies, one that recurs repeatedly in his work: the moment of insight points to the reality of a deeper isolation. As would be the case for Henry Fleming in *Red Badge*, Willie's revelations about the secret workings of the world in "An Experiment in Misery" intensifies, rather than alleviates, his sense of alienation. As was the case with *Maggie*, in "Misery"—which Crane gamely "researched" by dressing as a vagabond and wandering the streets at night—Crane's eye is tuned to the sociology of suffering; and it is here, perhaps—as in the above passage in which impersonal forces become "emblematic of a nation"—that he most clearly anticipates the naturalist mode of the writers like Frank Norris, Theodore Dreiser, and Jack London who would rise to prominence in the decade after Crane's death.

But is Stephen Crane himself to be regarded as a naturalist, like the writers mentioned above? Or a realist, working in the model established by Howells, Twain, and carried to new heights by Henry James and Edith Wharton? Might Crane be a proto-modernist, as Carl Van Doren suggested in 1924,[11] anticipating the elemental confrontations with death exhibited by his fellow newspaper-writer Ernest Hemingway? Perhaps a fourth term, like impressionist, is necessary—one that crosses some of these traditional generic boundaries. These questions have been remarkably persistent in Crane studies in the last century; and each argument, in its turn, is useful for *contextualizing* the range of representational strategies we find in Crane's work. Clearly, Crane came of age as a writer in the age of literary realism. In the period following the Civil War, the trend in American letters shifted from the imaginative, sometimes seemingly otherworldly, preoccupations of writers like Nathaniel Hawthorne, Ralph Waldo Emerson, and Herman Melville to a more focused commitment to depicting the world as it was. Mark Twain, and especially William Dean Howells—with his conviction that, in words reported by Crane for a highly stylized newspaper "interview" in 1894, "It is the business of the novel to picture the daily life in the most exact terms possible, with an absolute and clear sense of proportion"[12]—are usually seen as the foremost exemplars of the new approach. The street dialect Crane employed to such vivid effect in *Maggie*, and other tales, seems to recall Twain's earlier use of regional dialect in *Adventures of Huckleberry Finn*; but Crane was more conscious of the example of Howells. Announcing that he had "renounced the clever school in literature," Crane wrote to his friend Lily Brandon Munroe that he had developed a new approach: "Later I discovered that my creed was identical with the one of Howells and [Hamlin] Garland and in this way I became involved in the beautiful war between those who say that art is man's substitute for nature and we are the most successful in art when we approach nearest to nature and truth, and those who say—well, I don't know what they say. They don't, and can't say much. . . ."[13]

Aesthetic debates are perhaps a "beautiful war," but for Crane the approach "nearest to nature and truth" eschewed the contemplation of beauty as much as it disdained the "witty expedients" of "the clever school in literature." The opening scene of *Maggie*, which depicts the unwashed street urchin Jimmie defending the honor of Rum Alley in a rock-throwing fight atop a heap of gravel, situates truth in human conflict and nature in a barren landscape of human invention. Calibrating the relationship of "truth" to "nature" was for Crane the challenge of correct "proportion" identified by Howells as the test and signature of high realist art. In *Maggie*, a measure of truth is to be found in the baleful influence—not of Emerson's "Nature," writ large—but of a degraded social environment which is Nature's modern substitute. This equation for truth has a hard and bitter edge; in the tragic tale *Maggie*, Crane found an appropriately shocking vehicle to deliver it to the world. An inscription of a copy of *Maggie* to his friend, fellow realist Hamlin Garland reveals this ambitious purpose:

It is inevitable that you will be greatly shocked by this book but continue, please, with all possible courage to the end. For it tries to show that environment is a tremendous thing in the world and frequently shapes lives regardless. If one proves that theory, one makes room in Heaven for all sorts of souls (notably an occasional street girl) who are not confidently expected to be there by many excellent people.[14]

With his suggestion that the book "tries to show that environment is a tremendous thing in the world and frequently shapes lives regardless," Crane is uncharacteristically forthright in laying his philosophical cards on the table—elsewhere when talking about his work, he was always very careful to disclaim the presence of any "theories or pet ideas" in his fiction. "Preaching," he said, "is fatal to art and literature." As a realist, he felt it was his job "to give to readers a slice out of life; and if there is any moral or lesson in it I do not point it out. I let the reader find it for himself."[15] But in this private appraisal of *Maggie*, he gestures directly to a theory of environmental determinism. Not surprisingly, critics often key in on his note to Garland in order to explain Crane's philosophy as a writer—especially when the goal is to label Crane as an important early naturalist. If the aim of realism is to present life "as it is," without any potentially distorting commentary, naturalist writers—beginning with Émile Zola in the 1870s, with novels like *Nana*, but arriving in America only later—seek more explicitly to theorize the why and how. Following Zola, one might characterize naturalism as the application of the principles of scientific determinism to literature. The discoveries of thinkers like Marx, Darwin, and later Freud all suggest that humans act at the behest of forces they do not control—whether they are economic, evolutionary, or psychological. In France, Zola was the first to enlist such explanatory models as the basis of a new program for literature; but the pollination of these ideas did not make much of an impact in the United States until the turn of the century. Naturalists did not abandon the realist goal of being true to life—in fact, naturalist fiction often aspires to a kind of documentary accuracy in the service of proving the totalizing social theories that inspired them. At the same time, of course, an avowed commitment to one explanatory model is a form of limitation. Whereas a writer like Frank Norris would point to the deleterious effects of capitalism in novels like *McTeague* (1899) and *The Octopus* (1901) in the aid of social protest, a cruder form of evolutionary determinism—the rule of the survival of the fittest—would come to shape Jack London's work, particularly *The Call of the Wild* (1903) and *White Fang* (1906).

But Crane, unlike some of those who succeeded him (in addition to Norris, the "muckraking" fiction of Upton Sinclair comes to mind), was not chiefly a protest writer. Although stories like the Bowery Tales and "The Monster" reveal conditions of injustice, Crane is not principally concerned with political or social reform. Instead, Crane mines episodes of injustice for deeper ironies that speak to the precariousness and isolation of human experience. Nor did he commit himself to any one explanatory theory in his fiction.

Indeed, if Crane was able to avow that "environment is a tremendous thing and frequently shapes lives regardless," the example of his work as a whole seems to suggest that this statement is offered less as an explanation than as a testament to a kind of titanic and terrible awe. Nature—or its fallen social derivative—shapes lives without human regard because it is overwhelming, irresistible, and finally indifferent. Far from being reducible to any theory, "environment" is, in a word, *tremendous*—that is, monumental, something that inspires trembling and rebuffs explanation. Crane would agree with Henry Adams when he writes, "For human purposes a point must always be soon reached where the larger synthesis is suicide."[16] In one of Crane's better-known poems, from the volume *War is Kind* (1899), he eschews theoretical synthesis in favor of cosmological enigma:

A man said to the universe:
"Sir, I exist!"
"However," replied the universe,
"The fact has not created in me
"A sense of obligation."[17]

Everywhere there are signs of nature's unmistakable majestic power; but for Crane, experience is always stitched with the inescapable irony that the universe is finally indifferent to the fate of individuals. In Crane's stark, cryptic poems—which he preferred to his more famous and better-received novels and stories—such metaphysical quandaries predominate. In them, we may find a valuable means for addressing the stakes of his fiction. If his stories are preoccupied with conflict, depicting individuals at odds with each other and with the harsh realities of a hostile world, the metaphysical backdrop of stories like "The Open Boat," or "The Blue Hotel" has a certain alienating majesty in which—like the poem quoted above—the outcomes of individual dramas echo but fail to resonate with any higher purpose. As the narrator and Crane-surrogate of "The Open Boat" reflects, "When it occurs to a man that nature does not regard him as important, and that she feels she would not maim the universe by disposing of him, he at first wishes to throw bricks at the temple, and he hates deeply the fact that there are no bricks and no temples."[18]

The ambitions of Crane's characters are always edged with this grim irony, and are nowhere more vividly dramatized than in his masterpiece, *The Red Badge of Courage*. The novel opens at the scene of a Union encampment, twitching with impatient anticipation at rumors that the march to combat was imminent. As the narrative eye passes over the boisterous remarks of "the Tall Soldier" and "the Loud Soldier," it comes to rest on the contemplations of Crane's representative "youth", Private Henry Fleming.

"He had, of course, dreamed of battles all his life—of vague and bloody conflicts that had thrilled him with their sweep and fire. In visions he had seen himself in many struggles. He had imagined peoples secure in the shadow of his eagle-eyed prowess."[19] Henry arrives at war armed with Homeric dreams of heroism; but these visions of glory are made to dissolve instantly before the battle that seems "like the grinding of an immense and terrible machine to him," animated by mysterious "complexities and powers . . . [and] grim processes."[20] Massive, alien, industrial—the battle draws Henry with a wonder mixed with horror. Although it is clear that his romantic illusions of heroic distinction are made irrelevant in the face of its terrible power, it is less clear that Henry is able to replace those illusions with any reliable knowledge. As is the case in almost all of Crane's best fiction, ironic contrast is the key to an ambivalent insight: the "grim processes" of war will always resist analysis; and if Henry has "redeemed" his early cowardice by performing honorably in battle, the figure who emerges in its aftermath remains attached, though more shakily, to the adolescent dreams of grandeur and mastery with which he originally (and poorly) equipped himself for war.

Terrible violence—and death, its inescapable product—is the defining fact of life in *Red Badge*, and the ever-hovering possibility of its sudden eruption characterizes much of Crane's best work, such as "A Mystery of Heroism" (1895), and the Western stories, "Bride Comes to Yellow Sky" (1897) and "The Blue Hotel" (1899). And yet it is innocence, particularly the innocence of children, which frequently draws Crane's pen. A generation earlier, writers like Harriet Beecher Stowe used the suffering of children as a device, as a way of provoking outrage about conditions of injustice. In tales like "The Monster," and "A Dark-Brown Dog," Crane seems to work in the opposite direction. Violence and suffering are not questioned so much as they are presented as given facts of human existence, the result of accident or human caprice. What interests Crane is the ways in which these conditions illuminate the nature of a child's innocence through contrast—and thus reveal the high cost of what is lost when we fall from that innocence. But innocence is never pure for Crane's children; when the unnamed child at the center of "A Dark-Brown Dog" repeatedly strikes the stray dog he finds on the street; we understand that, like his father, he too is capable of wanton cruelties. Unlike adults, Crane's children are ignorant of the larger social and material contexts of violence and injustice. Instead, they are resilient and ever in earnest—they live entirely within the immediacy of their impressions and possess a serious, almost solemn curiosity about the worlds in which they live.

In "The Monster," these latter qualities are elevated to a near-mystical reverence before the spectacle of a house fire, or before the wrecked features of burn victim Henry Johnson. The eponymous "monster" of the tale, Henry Johnson had been the boon companion of young Jimmie, and is nearly killed while saving Jimmie from a terrible house fire. Alternately fearful of "the monster who lived above the carriage house," and transfixed by a "weird fascination," Jimmie is only able to bring himself to approach Johnson when goaded to do so by his friends. Emboldened by the dare, Jimmie affects the bravado of a carnival barker, and "seemed to reap all the joys of the owner and exhibitor of one of the world's marvels, while his audience remained at a distance—awed and entranced, fearful and envious."[21] Like the child's abuse of the dog, Jimmie's actions here are presented as something of a parable about childhood psychology; but each of these characters is blind to the larger implications of his actions. As readers we know that the cruelty of the child in "A Dark-Brown Dog" is acquired. More poignant still is the scene from "The Monster" related above: Henry Johnson is African-American; and though Jimmie is oblivious to the racial politics of casting himself as the *carnivalesque* "owner and exhibitor" of his erstwhile friend, the painful irony is not lost on the reader.

Crane's masterful 1897 story, "Death and the Child" further exploits the dramatic possibilities of childhood perspective by casting it amidst the cataclysmic theater of war he had so richly explored in *The Red Badge of Courage* three years earlier. Written following Crane's experiences as a newspaper correspondent covering the Greco-Turkish War, "Death and the Child" is, like *The Red Badge of Courage*, a drama of failed perspective; but here, the depth of Peza's disillusionment is made more startling and profound by the incongruous counterpoint of a child in the din of battle. Like Pvt. Henry Fleming, the protagonist of "Death and the Child" is an untried young man very much in earnest about realizing dreams of heroism in the defense of his fatherland. Greek by birth, Peza is an Italian correspondent sent to cover the war; but upon witnessing the plight of uprooted peasants, he chooses to take an active role. Wearing a conspicuous new white helmet and a new revolver, repeating his mantra to any who will listen, "Now I want to be a soldier. Now I want to fight," Peza passes from company to company amidst the escalating confusion and violence of the front. Crane masterfully depicts Peza's deepening panic by interweaving his narrative with that of an innocent little boy who, absorbed in the play of an imaginary game, is oblivious to the nature of the violence spreading beneath him. The story approaches its climax in a scene reminiscent of Henry Fleming's ghastly encounter with the dead man in the forest "chapel," in which Peza is overwhelmed by the terrible visage of a dead soldier. Crane delves into Peza's mind, depicting a psychology of terror in terms characteristic of much of his work:

> Peza could feel himself blanch; he was being drawn and drawn by these dead men slowly, firmly down as to some mystic chamber under the earth where they could walk, dreadful figures, swollen and blood-marked. He was bidden; they had commanded him; he was going, going, going.[22]

The inanimate takes on a terrifying depth, and the unknown province of death reveals itself as a commanding, irresistible force. Fleeing in terror, Peza scrambles up a cliff and collapses where, gasping, speechless, he is discovered by the boy. For the reader, the innocent, repeated question of the boy that closes the story "Are you a man?" throws Peza's naïve ambitions into an existential relief: no, he is emphatically less than the dream of soldierly manhood he had imagined; instead, a darker picture of "man" is revealed here, exposed and alone before the alienating mystery of death.

Such elemental encounters recur often in Crane's work, suspending dramatic progress in moments of frozen, open questioning. In "Death and the Child," a confrontation with death precipitates an alien encounter between man and child; in the chapel scene of *Red Badge*, the encounter is between man and corpse; and in the Western tale, "The Blue Hotel," the encounter is more alienated still—between corpse and machine. Having provoked his own murder at the hands of a gambler, "[t]he corpse of the Swede, alone in the saloon, had its eyes fixed upon a dreadful legend that dwelt a-top of the cash-machine: 'This registers the amount of your purchase.'"[23] Compare this scene to Henry Fleming's macabre moment of reckoning in the forest "chapel," in which "[h]e was being looked at by a dead man. . . . The eyes, staring at the youth, had changed to the dry, dull hue seen on a dead fish . . . He was for a few moments turned to stone before it. He remained staring into the liquid-looking eyes. The dead man and the living man exchanged a long look"[24] Suspended by the force of a gaze that uncannily mirrors his own, Henry Fleming's moment of self-discovery is staged here as a vanishing into oblivion. Striking, suggestive, and ultimately enigmatic—these scenes arrest character and reader alike. Such powerful encounters at the scene of death cast witnessing as a *transformative* act; but transformation here comes through self-estrangement, a kind of fall from innocence which neither act nor testimonial may restore. In the following poem, from *The Black Riders* (1895), Crane revisits this theme by casting the scene of the alien encounter onto a generic, inhospitable landscape:

> In the desert
> I saw a creature, naked, bestial,
> Who, squatting upon the ground,
> Held his heart in his hands,
> And ate of it.
> I said, "is it good, friend?"
> "It is bitter—bitter," he answered;
> "But I like it
> "Because it is bitter,
> "And because it is my heart."[25]

Here, Crane dramatizes an elemental confrontation with self as an act of cannibalism. The double-articulation of the question, "is it good"—that is, good to eat, or morally pure? Which is sustained, rather than resolved, by the creature's answer of "bitter." The ambiguous tone sounded here echoes repeatedly in Crane's fiction, as in the closing lines of "The Blue Hotel," in which the Easterner proclaims that all, and none, are guilty of the Swede's murder. Far from being the responsible party, the gambler who stabbed the Swede to death "isn't even a noun. He is kind of an adverb. Every sin is the result of a collaboration . . . you, I, Johnnie, old Scully, and that fool of an unfortunate gambler came merely as a culmination, the apex of a human movement, and gets all the punishment." [sic][26]

In *The Red Badge of Courage*, the nature of Crane's ambiguous moral thematic finds perhaps its most thorough dramatic realization. One of the chief difficulties in finding a center of ethical purpose within Henry Fleming's sphere of duty is that the failure of courage is presented far more vividly than the purpose and possibility of moral action. While it is clear that Henry attempts to "correct" for his cowardice by returning and living up to his commitment to his regiment, his successful performance in battle—the expiating act—does not amount to a test of his personal moral courage. Indeed, it is precisely here that "Henry" seems to vanish as a conscious, deliberative presence altogether. Caught up in the collective force of the troop advance, he becomes transformed into "an insane soldier."[27] The completeness of Fleming's surrender to the forces of battle is made explicit, somewhat ironically, in a scene in which he is a spectator. Even as "words of the new battle" raged, roaring out "a message of warning," Henry is shown (along with the lieutenant) to be delivering himself of unprecedented volleys of fiery language, speaking unconsciously, "prattling" gibberish and making "grotesque exclamations"—as if the battle has consumed them both and is marshaling them as organs of its own violent eruptions of voice.[28] Thus if Henry's "success" in battle begins when he permits himself to become the passive instrument of the battle-machine's collective destruction, his capacity to behave morally in human relationships remains uncertain at best. Recalling "the tattered man" and his "vivid error" at the close of the novel, he gradually musters the strength to "put the sin at a distance."[29] But the pervasive presence of Crane's irony makes it enormously difficult to diagnose the precise nature of the "change" Henry Fleming has undergone. For all of our privileged access to the vicissitudes of Henry's mind, we cannot be sure of the degree of his transformation, or of the extent of his learning. As Marston LaFrance suggests in his reading of *Red Badge*, "if moral values are to exist and man's life is to be meaningful, morality must be the creation of man's weak mental machinery alone."[30] The presence of the external world may be unpredictable, urgent, and horrifying; but in the end, it is external. Within an amoral universe, the context for human morality *must* begin with human invention—however unreliable our "mental machinery" may be.[31]

Predictably, the bulk of critical attention devoted to Crane's work has centered on *The Red Badge of Courage*, the most popular and best received of his works during his lifetime, and by far the most-read in the century since. Beginning with R.W. Stallman's energetic "revaluation" of *The Red Badge of Courage* in the 1950s, in which he reads the novel as Christian allegory, criticism of Crane's novel has tended toward polarization. While interpretive discussion has expanded gradually from debates over the meaning of Crane's infamous "pasted wafer" to more secular questions of irony—whether or not Pvt. Fleming's awakening to "new eyes" at the end of the book can be read as a positive self-realization—questions proceeding from Crane's impressionistic technique are often given peripheral interpretive importance. Some notable exceptions are offered by Milne Holton and James Nagel; and because of their inclusive concern for narrative structure, theirs are among the more insightful readings of *The Red Badge of Courage* available.

Stallman's reading hinges on the famous closing passage of chapter IX, which depicts the dying delirium of Henry's comrade, the "tall soldier" Jim Conklin. His final word, "God," transfixes Henry at this "ceremony" of death. "The youth turned, with sudden, livid rage, toward the battlefield. He shook his fist. He seemed about to deliver a philippic. / 'Hell—' / The red sun was pasted in the sky like a wafer."[32] "This grotesque image," writes Stallman, "[is] the most notorious metaphor in American literature."[33] Reading the vision of the pasted wafer an unmistakable sign of the Eucharist, Stallman suggests that Henry Fleming's redemption in battle lies along a spiritual path, and that his "red badge"—unlike the literal wound of Jim Conklin—"*is his conscience reborn and purified.*"[34] Although Stallman's allegorical reading of the novel has been much disputed, his critical work on Crane in the early 1950s marks an important turning point for scholarly study of Crane's work as a whole, and *Red Badge* in specific. Contemporary reviews often had praised the artistry of the book's succession of vivid episodes, or applauded Crane's "triumph of making us realize what Henry saw and heard as well as what he felt," as Harold Frederic wrote in early 1896.[35] But as Stallman points out, the novel is more than a stream of vivid episodes speaking to the eternal verities of war, fear, and courage; it is, indeed, a fully realized work of art and deserves to be treated as such.

Stallman's emphasis on structural unity and symbolic coherence reveal at once his allegiance to the techniques of New Criticism, then the dominant critical mode in the United States. As Donald Pizer points out, the approach Stallman advocated in the 1950s is to be contrasted with more naturalistic readings that developed around the same time. The difference, he explains, turns on an understanding of Crane's use of irony: "Was Crane ironic in his depiction of Henry's final self-estimation, or did he accept as valid Henry's judgment? An ironic reading led in the direction of a naturalistic interpretation of the novel; a reading of Henry's final self-examination as apt are led toward an acceptance of the themes of growth, development, and spiritual rebirth."[36] In other words, to read the narrative resolution of *Red Badge* as a spiritual rebirth along Christian lines, one must locate images like the "red sun pasted in the sky like a wafer" within a larger symbolic architecture that acts as a final guarantor of the novel's meaning, somewhere beyond the reeling vagaries of Henry Fleming's clouded mind and the "reality" of the battle itself.

But where are we to find this symbolic architecture? Like all of Crane's major works of fiction, *Red Badge* is written in the third person; but this exterior narrative perspective is never fully "outside" the mind of Henry Fleming. Instead, it is offered as a stylized refraction of Henry's consciousness. As Milne Holton usefully points out, "The fact which is so little understood about the novel is that in it Henry Fleming's and not Stephen Crane's imagination directly generate symbolic meanings."[37] Keying in on this central aspect of Crane's technique, James Nagel reads Crane not as a realist, symbolist, or naturalist, but as a literary impressionist. In this, Nagel is following in the footsteps of Ford Madox Ford and Joseph Conrad, the latter of whom once having hailed Crane as "*the* impressionist." Nagel writes, "[t]he purpose of Impressionistic writing is not polemical, often not even 'thematic' in the sense of organizing the details of fiction to point toward a predetermined idea, but rather to render the sensory nature of life itself, especially to make the reader 'see' the narrative described."[38] This version of impressionism refuses the "predetermined idea" that characterizes naturalistic scientism; but neither is it properly "realistic"— instead of striving to depict nature as it is, impressionism dwells on the sensory experience of it. In other words, Crane's "impressions" are preeminently psychological phenomena; they do not necessarily constitute a reliable record of reality. Thus "the reader is forced to exercise a continuous skepticism about the reliability of narrative assertions of judgment and of fact."[39]

Beyond these considerations, where issues of point-of-view become matters of philosophical and psychological positioning, the label of literary impressionism for Crane's work is helpful in illuminating his incorporation of painterly techniques in his writing. Crane's remarkable use of color— evident even in his titles, "The Blue Hotel," *The Red Badge of Courage*, "The Bride Comes to Yellow Sky," *The Black Riders*, and so on—betokens not only a philosophical concern with perception and its relation to truth, but also an abiding interest in the nature of visual experience. Experiences of places and objects are for Crane first and foremost visual experiences which, as in the vivid opening sentences of *George's Mother*, may already be distorted by tired conventions of their own: "In the swirling rain that came at dusk the broad avenue glistened with that deep bluish tint which is so widely condemned when it is put into pictures."[40] Instead of correcting for the visual cliché, Crane extends and deepens our experience of it, citing the "full, golden light" that shines from the shop windows, and the "flare of uncertain, wavering crimson" that is thrown from the street lamps onto the wet pavement. This type of exaggerated color play, in which each hue surreally enhances its referent, combines in a magnified aesthetic that takes us beyond the province of realism proper. Stallman has named this effect *prose pointillism*, a composition of "disconnected images, which coalesce like blobs of color in French impressionistic paintings,"[41] and it is often thought of as the result of a cross-pollination of ideas in 1892–93, when Crane lived in the Art Students' League in New York with artist friends like Corwin Knapp Linson, who later averred, "had not Stephen Crane been an artist in words he must have used color with a brush."[42]

More recent trends in Crane scholarship have situated his work within the larger historical dynamics of the 1890s, inquiring into the representational status of such things as science, technology, commodities, and public cultural rituals as a way of illuminating the signifying structures in Crane's work that correspond to everyday life. In his book, *Bodies and Machines*, Mark Seltzer uses Crane's stories as case studies for tracking the cultural preoccupation with numbers and statistics as theoretical models for urban life that came to the fore in the latter part of the 19th century. Devoting particular attention to *Maggie*, Seltzer suggests that Crane's stories participate in a larger cultural logic embodied in the realist mode of representation—one obsessed with seeing, statistics, and the relationship between people's bodies and social spectacle. At the heart of realism, he claims, is "a desire to make visible: to embody, physically or materially, character, persons, and inner states and, collaterally, to 'open' these states to what Crane calls the 'machines of perception.'"[43] Hence Maggie's keen fascination with the ventriloquist and his twin marionettes, or with the melodramatic stage actress she sees in her trip to the theater with Pete. Maggie wonders if the "culture and refinement" she had seen onstage was something that "could be acquired by a girl who lived in a tenement house and worked in a shirt factory." For Maggie, the contents of personhood are not only visual, they are potentially exchangeable as well; Seltzer sees in her belief in the improving potential of imitation a desire not only to transcend her material conditions, but a particular way of understanding individual identity itself. Rather than something that is understood to be private and interior, the most important values of personhood are those that are legible to others in public display. Paradoxically, argues Seltzer, "the desire to see that marks Crane's stories, the aesthetic and erotic fascination with a vision that is also a supervision, always implicitly calls forth its opposite: . . . the very absorption in, even intoxication with, seeing opens the possibility of violent loss of balance or *dis*empowerment."[44] In other words, the privileging of a publicly visible identity carries great risk when, as in Maggie's case; one's public reputation is damaged. Hence the pervasive presence of the prostitute in realist texts like *Maggie*: "this is because the case of the fallen girl provides a way of at once embodying . . . the desire to see and the project of making 'the social' visible."[45]

In his book, *The Material Unconscious: American Amusement, Stephen Crane, & the Economies of Play*, Bill Brown offers a fresh context for reading Crane by mapping the rituals and material objects of public recreation—games and sports, amusement parks, freak shows—that intersect in Crane's work. Like Seltzer, Brown does not focus on Crane's work as an interpretive end-in-itself; instead, Brown uses Crane to tell a story of the American 1890s, "wherein the problems and possibilities of the recreational assume pivotal importance in the way Americans conceive and experience their daily lives and public selves."[46] In "American Childhood and Stephen Crane's Toys," Brown focuses on Crane's Whilomville Stories, in particular "The Stove," in an effort to track the ways in which mass-produced toys locate the representation of children on a cultural continuum that connects idyllic myths of childhood innocence with the rise of consumer culture. "On the one hand, these stories participate in a national(izing) production of the child, performed by both the boy's book and the child study movement, which *spatialize* play as a timeless utopia."[47] At the same time, Brown argues, the presence of the stove in the story records the incursion of market commodities into that utopian space—which is precisely what empowers the girl in the story "to enter and disrupt the world of boys." Brown goes on to suggest that this scenario stages a fundamental tension about market culture often glossed over in contemporary materialist criticism: "Although arguments about the unifying myths of America have now been supplanted by arguments about how consumer culture itself effects a 'national life,' Crane's story shows precisely how such myths and consumer culture came into conflict."[48]

Some of the most interesting and important Crane scholarship in the last twenty years has been in the field of Crane biography, following revelations that, as Christopher Benfey puts it, "for seven decades much of the scholarship on Crane's life and work has been based on a fraud."[49] That "fraud" is the first Crane biography to have appeared after his death, Thomas Beer's 1923 volume, *Stephen Crane: A Study in American Letters*. According to his colleague Wilson Follett, Beer—who idolized Crane—was possessed of an unusually active imagination. "He could quote pages verbatim from authors who never wrote any such pages; sometimes from authors who never lived. He could rehearse the plots of stories never written by their ostensible authors, or by anybody, repeat pages of dialogue from them, and give you the (nonexistent) places and dates of publication."[50] It is now clear that many of the "facts" of Crane's life presented originally by Beer—and reproduced in subsequent biographies by John Berryman (1950) and R. W. Stallman (1968)—simply cannot be documented; and many of the famous letters he quotes have been uncovered as forgeries. Indeed, the impressive scholarly detective work of Paul Sorrentino and Stanley Wertheim suggests that the authenticity of more than *sixty* of the letters Beer "quotes" must be questioned, if not refused outright as disingenuous.

Into this vacuum three major new works have appeared—Christopher Benfey's critical biography *The Double Life of Stephen Crane* (1992); Wertheim and Sorrentino's indispensable *The Crane Log: A Documentary Life of Stephen Crane*; and, most recently, Linda Davis's *Badge of Courage: The Life of Stephen Crane* (1998). As Benfey suggests, the movement of Crane's life with regard to his work carries a special fascination for the biographer. "If most writers tend to write about their experience, however disguised, Crane did the reverse: he tried to live what he'd already written."[51] Thus we are faced with *Maggie*, a tale of prostitution which precedes Crane's own affair with the southern madam Cora Taylor; or *The Red Badge of Courage*, the imaginative projection of battle written by one who had not experienced it, preceding Crane's own journey as a war-correspondent to Greece to see if he got it right.[52]

But if Crane seemed compelled to capture in life the intensity of moments he modeled first on the page, the conclusions in his work suggest that those experiences are, in essence, too powerful to handle. When we read Henry Fleming's famous estimation of the day's battle at the end of *Red Badge*—"He had been to touch the great death, and found that, after all, it was but the great death"—we understand that it is not an honest reckoning of the experience, but the effort of a besieged mind to put the trauma of death at a distance. Indeed, reading Crane's work within the narrative arc of his life, it is impossible not to return to the recurring topic of death—that great theme of his fiction that also marked the early eclipse of his earthly career. Remembering her 1895 meeting with Crane, Willa Cather succumbs to the temptation of reading the two as somehow mysteriously related. His eyes, she writes—"the finest I have ever seen, large and dark and full of lustre and changing lights"—are in her memory filled with a "profound melancholy" and "seemed to be burning themselves out." His mood discouraged and his health failing, "[h]e went about with the tense, preoccupied air of a man who is brooding over some impending disaster."[53] In Cather's vivid depiction, one senses less a true picture of Stephen Crane as he was than a picture of Cather's own memory, transformed by her knowledge of his eventual and premature death. This is perhaps a distortion of the "true" Stephen Crane; but if so then Crane's fiction suggests that it is also an inevitable one, born of a habit of vision we all share. As we continue to read Crane's work, we might recall a wry comment he made to his editor: "I cannot help vanishing and disappearing and dissolving. It is my foremost trait." As the figure of Crane the author vanishes into his work, the power of his achievement ensures the richness of his perpetual reemergence, in new contexts, for new generations of readers.

NOTES

1. Henry James to Cora Taylor Crane, 7 June 1900, *The Correspondence of Stephen Crane*. Ed. Stanley Wertheim and Paul Sorrentino. 2 Vol. (New York: Columbia University Press, 1988), II. 659.

2. William Dean Howells to Cora Taylor, 29 July 1900, *Stephen Crane: The Critical Heritage*, ed. Richard Weatherford (London: Routledge & Kegan Paul, 1973), 60.

3. *Stephen Crane: The Critical Heritage*, 336.

4. *Stephen Crane: The Critical Heritage*, 332.

5. Cf. Edwin H. Cady, *Stephen Crane*, rev. ed. (Boston: G.K. Hall-Twayne, 1980), 119.

6. Stephen Crane to Ripley Hitchcock, 15? March 1896, *The Correspondence of Stephen Crane*, I.213.

7. Henry Adams, *The Education of Henry Adams* (Boston: Houghton Mifflin, 1961), 331.

8. Ibid., 343.

9. Stephen Crane, "An Experiment in Misery," *Stephen Crane: Prose and Poetry* (New York: Library of America, 1984), 548.

10. Stephen Crane, *Maggie: A Girl of the Streets (A Story of New York)*,1893. Ed. Thomas A. Gullason (New York: Norton Critical Edition, 1979), 53.

11. Carl Van Doren, *American Mercury*, Jan. 1924, i.: 11–14, Rpt. in *Stephen Crane: The Critical Heritage*, ed. Richard Weatherford (London: Routledge & Kegan Paul, 1973), 326.

12. Stephen Crane, "Fears Realists Must Wait," *New York Times*, 28 October 1894: 20. Rpt. in *Uncollected Writings*, ed. Olov W. Fryckstedt. (N.P.: Uppsala, 1963), 80.

13. Stephen Crane to Lily Brandon Munroe, March/April 1894, *The Correspondence of Stephen Crane*, I. 63.

14. Ibid., I. 53.

15. Stephen Crane to the editor of *Demorest's Family Magazine*, May 1896, *The Correspondence of Stephen Crane*, I. 230.

16. *The Education of Henry Adams*, 402.

17. *Stephen Crane: Prose and Poetry* (New York: Library of America, 1984), 1335.

18. Stephen Crane, "The Open Boat" (1898), *The Red Badge of Courage and Other Writings*, ed. Richard Chase (Boston: Riverside-Hougton Mifflin, 1960), 306.

19. Stephen Crane, *The Red Badge of Courage and Other Writings*, ed. Richard Chase (Boston: Riverside-Houghton Mifflin, 1960), 117.

20. Ibid., 158.

21. Stephen Crane, "The Monster" (1899), *The Red Badge of Courage and Other Writings*, ed. Richard Chase (Boston: Riverside-Houghton Mifflin, 1960), 367.

22. Stephen Crane, "Death and the Child" (1897), *Stephen Crane: Prose and Poetry* (New York: Library of America, 1984), 961.

23. Stephen Crane, "The Blue Hotel" (1899), *Stephen Crane: Prose and Poetry* (New York: Library of America, 1984), 826.

24. *Red Badge*, 155–56.

25. *Stephen Crane: Prose and Poetry* (New York: Library of America, 1984), 1299.

26. "The Blue Hotel," 827–28.

27. *Red Badge*, 205.

28. Ibid., 221.

29. Ibid., 230.

30. Marston LaFrance, "Private Fleming: His Various Battles," *A Reading of Stephen Crane* (Oxford: Oxford-Clarendon, 1971), 98.

31. Ibid.

32. Ibid., 165.

33. R. W. Stallman, "Stephen Crane: A Revaluation," *Critiques and Essays on Modern Fiction, 1920–1951*, ed. John W. Aldridge (New York: Ronald Press, 1952), 252–269. Rpt. in *Critical Essays on Stephen Crane's* The Red Badge of Courage, ed. Donald Pizer (Boston: G.K. Hall, 1990), 58.

34. Ibid., 57.

35. Harold Frederic, *New York Times*, Jan. 26 1896, 22. *Stephen Crane: The Critical Heritage*, ed. Richard Weatherford (London: Routledge & Kegan Paul, 1973), 118.

36. Donald Pizer, "Introduction," *Critical Essays on* The Red Badge of Courage (Boston: G.K. Hall, 1990), 6.

37. Milne Holton, *Cylinder of Vision: The Fiction and Journalistic Writing of Stephen Crane* (Baton Rouge: Louisiana State University Press, 1972), 91.

38. James Nagel, *Stephen Crane and Literary Impressionism* (University Park: Pennsylvania State University Press), 21.

39. Ibid.

40. Stephen Crane, *George's Mother*, *The Red Badge of Courage and Other Writings*, 62.

41. Robert. W. Stallman, *Stephen Crane: An Omnibus* (New York: Knopf, 1961), 185.

42. C.K. Linson, *My Stephen Crane*, ed. Edwin H. Cady (Syracuse NY: Syracuse UP, 1958), 32. Quoted in Nagel, *Stephen Crane and Literary Impressionism*, 16.

43. Mark Seltzer, "Statistical Persons," *Bodies and Machines* (New York: Routledge, 1992), 95.

44. Ibid., 96–97.

45. Ibid., 98–99.

46. Bill Brown, "Introduction," *The Material Unconscious: American Amusement, Stephen Crane, & the Economies of Play* (Cambridge MA: Harvard University Press, 1996), 4.

47. Ibid., 25.

48. Ibid.

49. Christopher Benfey, *The Double Life of Stephen Crane* (New York: Alfred A. Knopf, 1992), 7.

50. Wilson Follett to E. R. Hagemann, 12 April 1962, Quoted in Wertheim, Stanley and Paul Sorrentino, "Introduction," *The Correspondence of Stephen Crane*, ed. Wertheim and Sorrentino (New York: Columbia University Press, 1988), 7.

51. *The Double Life of Stephen Crane*, 5.

52. Ibid.

53. Willa Cather, *The World and the Parish: Willa Cather's Articles and Reviews, 1893–1902*, ed. William M. Curtin, 2 Vol. (Lincoln: University of Nebraska press, 1970), 772–74.

ROBERT WOOSTER STALLMAN

Stephen Crane: A Revaluation*₁

I

Stephen Crane is frequently spoken of as the most legendary figure in American letters since Edgar Allan Poe. A whole mythology of bizarre tales (some of them not entirely untrue) surrounds his elusive and enigmatic personality, and it is difficult to distinguish the real Crane from the mythical Crane when so much of the factual is itself fantastic. The fantastic pursued him beyond the grave in the fact that when he died his wife—an extraordinary woman and a faithful wife—returned to her former trade in Jacksonville, Florida, where as the madame of a bawdy house she presided over a mansion modeled upon Brede Place, the semi-medieval residence of the Cranes in England. Crane, by nature over-generous, had an immense capacity for friendship, which he shared equally with defeated failures—Bowery bums and streetwalkers—and with the literary great, Conrad and Henry James and Ford Madox Ford. Conrad affectionately attended him during his fatal illness, and Henry James, waiting upon him with over-solicitous devotion, treated him as though he were another Keats—a pet lamb in a sentimental tragedy. He lived violently and he died young, but even while he lived the real Crane was being converted into the conventional legend of the artist—luckless, penniless, creative only when fever-ridden or drunk. There is this folk version of the wayward genius, under which Crane's

From *Critiques and Essays on Modern Fiction, 1920–1951*, ed. John W. Aldridge. © 1952 The Ronald Press Company. Reprinted with permission.

myth-making personality has been likened to Poe's, and there is the more classical version of the "stricken boy," the genius who dies young— Chatterton, Keats, Schubert, Beardsley.

When we approach the work of Crane we are instantly struck by the impact of his greatness, and we marvel not only at that quite inexplicable uniqueness of his technique and style but also that so much in so short a span as eight writing years could be produced by a mere boy who, dying at twenty-eight, left behind him more than enough perfections to place him solidly among the half-dozen major artists of American fiction in the 19th Century—not in the first rank with Hawthorne and Melville and Henry James but, counting work for work, in the second rank with Poe and Howells and Twain. Crane perfected as many works in fiction as Twain and Poe—at his best in a half-dozen stories and one novel—*The Narrative of A. Gordon Pym*. Luckless in everything else, Crane had the great luck—phenomenal among writers—to write two works of art having major importance in American letters and to write them before he was twenty-two. He first broke new ground with *Maggie: A Girl of the Streets*, the then sordid realism of that work initiating the literary trend of the next generation. *Maggie* is a tone painting rather than a realistic photograph of slum life, but it opened the door to the Norris–Dreiser–Farrell school of sociological realism. In *The Red Badge of Courage* and "The Open Boat," that flawless construct of paradox and symbol, Crane established himself among the foremost technicians in American fiction. "The Open Boat" is a perfect fusion of the impressionism of *Maggie* and the symbolism of *The Red Badge of Courage*. The two main technical movements in modern American fiction—realism and symbolism— have their beginnings here in these early achievements of Stephen Crane.

What killed Crane was not literary neglect—he died, so the popular notion has it, "tragically young"; "a boy, spiritually killed by neglect"—but rather it was his own will to burn himself out, his Byronic craving to make his body "a testing ground for all the sensations of life." He aimed not to live very long (35 at best, so he told a friend) and, knowing that his time was short—he had no time to lose! He lived in desperation against time. Like F. Scott Fitzgerald, who wrote (to quote Malcolm Cowley) "in a room full of clocks and calendars," time was what Crane feared. Dying at the same sinister hour as Fitzgerald, at three in the morning, his life was again like Fitzgerald's in this: though filled with adventure, it was neither thrilling nor romantic but actually somewhat banal. "Even his war adventures," as H. L. Mencken says, "were far less thrilling in fact than in his florid accounts of them.

Crane was intense, volatile, spontaneous—what he wrote came un-watched from his pen. He wrote as he lived, and his life was shot through with ironies. If he won any "grace" from that "cold voyage" it was, I think, the artist's gift of ironic outlook, that grace of irony which is so central to his art. Irony is Crane's chief technical instrument. It is the key to our understanding of the man and of his works. He wrote with the intensity of a poet's emotion, the compressed emotion which bursts into symbol and paradox. All his best works are built upon paradox. They are formed upon ironic contrasts between ideals or romantic illusions *and* reality.

Actually, Crane wasted his genius. Under the mistaken notion that only those who have suffered shipwreck can become its interpreters, he expended himself in a misspent search for experience. Wilfully and needlessly he risked his life—among bandits in Mexico, under shellfire in Cuba and Greece as war correspondent, and off the Florida seacoast as a filibustering seaman in the disaster which befell him when he survived shipwreck after suffering thirty hours at sea in a ten-foot dinghy. It was natural that Crane should want to see actual warfare after writing about it, and four years later as war correspondent in the Graeco-Turkish War he tested the psychological truth of his imagined picture. "My picture was all right!" he told Conrad. "I have found it as I imagined it." But at what a cost! Exposures endured in Cuba wrecked his health and impaired his art—nothing vital came from his war experience. And the pity of it all is that it could have been otherwise. He could have lived in one of his brothers' homes and done his writing there. He could have retreated from life to calculate it at a distance, as Hawthorne and James did. Instead, he deliberately chose to get as close to life as possible.

He wanted to get at the real thing and so he stood all night in a blizzard, in order to write "Men in the Storm"; to get at the real thing he spent a night in a Bowery flophouse in order to write "An Experiment in Misery"; to get at the real thing he traveled across the Western prairies, and out of it he got "The Blue Hotel" and "The Bride Comes to Yellow Sky"; out of Mexico he got "Horses—One Dash!" and other sketches; and out of Cuba and Greece impressions of war for *Wounds in the Rain*, stories like "Death and the Child" and the novel *Active Service*. But was there any need for Crane to experience a blizzard in order to write "Men in the Storm"? Wouldn't an imaginary rather than an actual blizzard have served just as well, since the germinal idea of the story is about a *symbolic* storm—the storm of social strife? Familiarizing himself with New York tenement life certainly wasn't necessary for the germinal idea of "An Auction," in which he depicts the social shame of a poor couple whose household goods are auctioned off amidst the derisive mockery of a parrot and a gaping crowd. No personal experience of Bret Harte's country was needed to write parodies of Bret Harte's Californian tales—in "Moonlight in the Snow," "Twelve O'Clock," and "A Self Made Man." Much of Crane's anecdotal material might just as well have originated in the experience of others, and in fact some of it did—for example, the incident used in "The Lone Charge of Francis B. Perkins" was taken from Ralph Paine.

Crane excels in the portrayal of mental turmoil, and for this psychological realism his creative imagination required no firsthand experience. His most directly autobiographical tales are "The Open Boat" and "Horses— One Dash!" "The Open Boat" is a direct transcript of personal experience, but it is personal experience transformed into an impersonal and symbolic representation of life: the plight of man tossed upon in indifferent sea. Crane transcribed it all from his experience, but he converted every detail into symbol, designed every image into a schemework of relationships, and manipulated the original facts and their sequence to form a patterned whole, a construct possessing a life of its own. He created his facts into patterns of contrast—the men in the dinghy *and* the people on the shore, the *white* and the *black* waves, the *sea* and the *land*, etc.—and he converted them into symbols—*viz.* the oar of the oiler, the windmill, etc. The only source that explains the calculated design and patterned significance of "The Open Boat" is the conceiving imagination of the artist.

His two greatest works represent two opposite methods of creation: art created from imagined experience and art created from actual experience. The single marvel he wrung from actual experience was "The Open Boat," and the marvel of it is that he at once transcribed life and converted it into art. Yet a paradox is here established, for the masterpiece which he salvaged from his expense of greatness (as Gorham Munson was first to point out) could have been conceived without any personal experience—as *The Red Badge of Courage* is there to testify. Crane's best works do not vindicate or support the creative principle by which they were generated.

There is thus an ironic contradiction between Crane's theory of creation and his art. His infrequent comments about art—oblique hints given out in an offhand air—amount to no more than the singlestick standard of sincerity and truth to the facts of experience. "My creed was identical with the one of Howells and Garland," he wrote in a letter of 1896. The creed of veritism which Hamlin Garland preached, the theory that art is founded upon personal experience and is copyistic of reality, Crane echoed when, not long before his death, he told a friend: "You can never do anything good aesthetically . . . unless it has at one time meant something important to you." His theory was that the greater the artist the closer his contact with reality. Yet his art was at its greatest when he wrote at some distance from the reality he had experienced, or when (as in "The Upturned Face" and "An Episode of War") he wrote out of no personal experience at all.

In his quest for and immersion in experience Crane stands at the headstream of what has been defined as the dominant American theme and literary trend—exemplified in Ernest Hemingway, Sherwood Anderson, and Thomas Wolfe, who put the same premium upon personal experience. At his best Crane used not the experienced event but the event distilled for the thematic potentialities it suggested. The exception is "The Open Boat," but here—as with Conrad in his "Heart of Darkness," which is taken straight from life—the personal experience served simply as the canvas for the recreated picture. For Crane and Conrad alike, contacts with reality provided hints for characters, details of locality, themes and germinal situations. But Crane seldom presents minute descriptions of people or scenes, and details of locality are not photographically recorded. The locality of "The Blue Hotel" has symbolic import and could have been sketched without firsthand experience of it. Crane could have written it without leaving New York City. The fight which he witnessed and tried to stop during his trip west (when in Lincoln, Nebraska) became the fight which he depicted in "The Blue Hotel," but the germinal idea for the story might just as well have had a literary source instead of this personal one. "The Blue Hotel," though it has been labeled a Hemingway story, is identical in germinal conception with Robert Louis Stevenson's formula: a certain scene and atmosphere suggest the correlative action and persons for that particular locality, and they are so used as to express and symbolize it. The atmosphere of the old blue hotel, the psychic quality of its screaming blue, impels and foreshadows the action which expresses the murder of the Swede.

It was realism that Crane aimed at—a photographic copy of real life. But Crane is, in essence, no realist. He believed, like Chekhov, that his task was to show persons and things as they really are, yet the persons of his fiction are not persons but just Everyman—the synthetic figures of a Morality Play or a medieval tapestry, the typical representatives of a group (the young soldier from the farm, the Bowery bum, the cowboy). In "A Self Made Man," for example, we get a character called Thomas G. Somebody. Crane was always symbolizing. Henry Fleming, being a more sensitive and imaginative person than the ordinary soldier, is not solely a type (as George Wyndham, in a preface to a collection of Crane's war stories, was first to point out). One might argue that all of Crane's characters have certain marked idiosyncracies which set them apart from the type they represent, yet types they are as well as individuals. If there is any one point of common agreement among Crane's critics, it is the point that Crane in presenting a character (to quote Bushman's summing up) "was *always* at the same time dealing with generalities. . . . His characters are *representatives*; they are individuals *and* representatives of large groups."

Next to Ambrose Bierce, who despised realism (but not in his own war tales), Crane attained a reputation greater than any other American writer about war. What Crane wrote still passes as "real war literature," yet neither Crane nor Bierce rendered the actualities of recruits under fire with anything like the graphic and authentic realism of J. W. De Forest. Crane did not write our first realistic war novel (most Crane critics and historians credit him with that). De Forest's work appeared long before Crane's *Red Badge of Courage*. Nor did Crane write, as some critics have said, our first ironic novel. Neither *Maggie* nor *The Red Badge*, but Twain's *Huckleberry Finn* deserves that claim. Beside De Forest's "First Time Under Fire" and his novel *Miss Ravenel's Conversion*, Crane's imagined account of battlefields appears somewhat synthetic and even theatrical. Crane's realism differs from the realism of Zola and Norris: it is not photographic and documentary. Crane uses the devices of realism (as Wright Morris recently remarked) "for revelatory purposes. The *charge* of the writing is always more important than the literal content." In his best works Crane uses only so much realistic detail as his symbolic intent requires, that but no more. He is commonly credited with being the forerunner of realism in America, but the truth about *The Red Badge of Courage*, as William Phillips says, is that "this novel is realistic only in a thematic sense, for its style and sensibility have little in common with the method of additive detail associated with the modern realistic school."

II

The Red Badge of Courage was the first nonromantic novel of the Civil War to attain widespread popularity and, appearing at a time when war was still treated primarily as the subject for romance, it turned the tide of the prevailing convention and established a new if not unprecedented one. In style and method Crane had no predecessors, but in viewing war from the vantage point of the unromantic and commonplace conscript he was following the line set down by Walt Whitman, whose *Specimen Days* is our first modern approach to the subject; he was anticipated by Tolstoy, whose *Sevastopol* and *War and Peace* are realistic accounts of the tragedy of the rank and file in the Napoleonic and Crimean Wars;[2] and he was indebted to Colonel Wilbur F. Hinman, whose fictionalized reminiscences of the American Civil War, in *Corporal Si Klegg and His "Pard,"* portray the everyday life of the civilian soldier.

As for Crane influences, it has been claimed that Tolstoy's *Sevastopol* exerted a powerful influence on the conception of *The Red Badge of Courage*, and, by another critic, that but for Tolstoy it would never have been written. Yet no palpable debts can be established. Other source-hunters have thought of Stendhal's battle scenes as the model for Crane's, but Crane never read *La Chartreuse de Parme* and was angered when told that he had. He is supposed to have written *The Red Badge of Courage* on the dare of a friend to do better than Zola, whose tragedy of the Franco-Prussian War is recorded in *La Débâcle*, which Crane sometime before writing his novel dipped into but never finished. Zola bored him. he disliked Zola's statistical realism, and he disliked Tolstoy's panoramic method, finding "Peace and War" (as he called it) tiresome: "He could have done the whole business in one third the time and made it just as wonderful. It goes on and on like Texas." Tolstoy's *Anna Karenina* and Flaubert's *Salammbô* he resented on the same grounds. Even his own *The Red Badge of Courage* he criticized for the same reason: it was too long.

Crane confessed that he had read the French realists, but it is probable that he absorbed them only through translations and from Henry James's criticism of the French novelists. Essentially uneducated, he was not a bookish man. "His reading was miscellaneous, desultory, and unguided.[3] In general he disliked the writers of his time whom it was the fashion to like— including Stevenson." He judged literature and people by the criterion of sincerity and, hating the literary dandy, he detested Stevenson—the very man he himself most nearly resembled. Both are mannered writers, addicted to the word, stylists *par excellence*; both, limited in their range, write on similar fields of experience and out of childhood reminiscences. And each personality stirred up the legend of the artist. Both men were nomadic, magnetic, charming and chivalrous, plagued by ill-health; and they resembled each other not only in temperaments but in picturesque exteriors—each wore, as it were, the same absurd mustache.

The whole question of Crane influences is very difficult to pin down. It is debatable whether Crane took over anything out of his French and Russian readings. Most of these so-called influences are in fact (I think) nothing more than parallelisms. It is true that the formula for his short stories parallels the Flaubert–Maupassant–Turgenev formulae (as F. M. Ford pointed), but this much Crane could just as readily have taken over from Ambrose Bierce. In form and theme or subject, Bierce's affinities with Maupassant are the same as Crane's. Bierce's "An Occurrence at Owl Creek Bridge" and Crane's "The Upturned Face" have the same structural design as Maupassant's bitter war story "La Mère Sauvage": They have the form of a single mood, they are patterned upon an ironic contrast, they turn upon a central paradox. Bierce casts his stories at a distance from ordinary life and he romanticizes life by employing melodramatic movie-thriller plots, but (like Crane) he invests his war pictures with a conviction of visual reality. Their short stories are alike in form, in subject (children and the untried soldier), in theme (e.g., conscience and courage), in their use of chance or coincidence, and with different emphasis, in tone and emotional tension. Not only in their fiction but in their parable poetry there is a very close kinship between Bierce and Crane.

Crane's originality had its ancestry in his readings—the Bible, Bierce, Kipling, Poe, Twain, Tolstoy, etc.—and in what he inherited from experiences on the diamond and the gridiron—"I got my sense of the rage of conflict on the football field, or else fighting is a hereditary instinct, and I wrote intuitively. . . ." As Shakespeare's *Tempest* had its source in tavern-talk about a shipwreck off the Bermudas, so Crane's *Red Badge of Courage* had its source in conversations with veterans of the Civil War: the reminiscences of his brother, William, who was an expert in the strategy of Chancellorsville, and the tactical accounts of battle which Crane got from General Van Petten, his teacher at the Claverack Academy, the Hudson River Institute where he was schooled and drilled. Crane studied, furthermore, some of the contemporary accounts of the Civil War—the four volumes of The Century's *Battles and Leaders of the Civil War*, which were written almost exclusively by veterans, Harper's *History*, and Matthew Brady's remarkable photographs. But above all these readings he drew chiefly from Colonel Hinman's *Corporal Si Klegg and His "Pard"* (1887). Colonel Hinman's book was, I think, almost certainly Crane's primary literary source. But we are still left wondering where he learned *how* to write. The answer to that question is given, I believe, in Hemingway's remark: "I learned to write looking at paintings at the Luxembourg Museum in Paris."

Crane knew Ryder personally and he knew not only Ryder's paintings but some of Monet's, and Frederic Remington's drawings, and he had Brady's poignant photographs to brood over, Coffin's illustrations to *Si Klegg*, and the apprenticeship paintings of Corwin Linson and Crane's fellow-lodgers at the "Art Students' League," where he lived during the period when he was composing his own impressionistic paintings: *Maggie* and *The Red Badge of Courage*. A recent critic contends that Crane borrowed nothing of his technique from paintings, and here again it is difficult to establish proof of positive influence. I don't think the influence of the studio on Crane can be denied. The critically relevant point, however, is that there is a close parallelism between Crane's impressionistic prose and impressionistic painting. As H. G. Wells concluded in his essay of 1900: "there is Whistler even more than there is Tolstoy in *The Red Badge of Courage*."

Crane's style has been likened to a unique instrument which no one after his death has ever been able to play. *The Red Badge of Courage* seems unprecedented and noncomparable. But Chekhov, who was almost of an age with Crane, and a little later Katherine Mansfield, who adopted the method of Chekhov, were both masters of the same instrument. In its episodic structure and impressionistic style Chekhov's *The Cherry Orchard* suggests a legitimate parallel to *The Red Badge of Courage*. All three artists had essentially the same literary aim and method: intensity of vision and objectivity in rendering it. All three aimed at a depersonalization of art: they aimed to get outside themselves completely in order "to find the greatest truth of the idea" and "see the thing as it really is"; to keep themselves aloof from their characters, not to become emotionally involved with their subjects, and to comment on them not by statement but by evocation in picture and tone ("sentiment is the devil," said Crane, and in this he was echoing Flaubert).

Crane stands also in close kinship to Conrad and Henry James, the masters of the impressionist school. All these writers aimed to create (to use Henry James's phrase) "a direct impression of life." Their credo is voiced by Conrad in his celebrated Preface to "The Nigger of the 'Narcissus'"—it is "by the power of the written word, to make you hear, to make you feel—it is, before all, to make you *see*." Their aim was to immerse the reader in the created experience, so that its impact on the reader would occur simultaneously with the discovery of it by the characters themselves. Instead of panoramic views of a battlefield, Crane paints not the whole scene but disconnected segments of it, which, accurately enough, is all that a participant in an action or a spectator of a scene can possibly take into his view at any one moment. "None of them knew the colour of the sky"—that famous opening sentence of "The Open Boat"—defines the restricted point of view of the four men in the wave-tossed dinghy, their line of vision being shut off by the menacing walls of angry water. Busy at the oars, they knew the color of the sky only by the color of the sea and "they knew it was broad day because the colour of the sea changed from slate to emerald-green, streaked with amber lights, and the foam was like tumbling snow." Everything is keyed in a state of tension—even their speech, which is abrupt and composed of "disjointed sentences." Crane's style is itself composed of disjointed sentences, disconnected sense-impressions, chromatic vignettes by which the reality of the adventure is evoked in all its point-present immediacy.

Crane anticipated the French Post-Impressionist painters. *His style is*, in brief, *prose pointillism*. It is composed of disconnected images which, like the blobs of color in a French Impressionist painting, coalesce one with another, every word-group having a cross-reference relationship, every seemingly disconnected detail having interrelationship to the configurated pattern of the whole. The intensity of a Crane tale is due to this patterned coalescence of disconnected things, everything at once fluid and precise.

A striking analogy is established between Crane's use of colors and the method employed by the Impressionists and the Neo-Impressionists or

Divisionists, and it is as if he had known about their theory of contrasts and composed his own prose paintings by the same principle. It is the principle, as defined by the scientist Chevreul in his *Laws of Simultaneous Contrast*, that "Each plane of shade creates around itself a sort of aura of light, and each luminous plane creates around itself a zone of shade. In a similar way a coloured area communicates its 'complimentary' to the neighbouring colour, or heightens it if it is complimentary.'"[4] In almost every battle scene Crane paints in *The Red Badge of Courage*, the perspective is blurred by smoke or by the darkness of night. Here is one example of the former contrast, namely dark masses circled by light, and of the latter contrast, namely a luminous spot circled by darkness.

> The clouds were tinged an earthlike yellow in the sunrays and in the shadow were a sorry blue. The flag was sometimes eaten and lost in this mass of vapor, but more often it projected, sun-touched, resplendent. (Page 77.)*

Crane's perspectives, almost without exception, are fashioned by contrasts—black masses juxtaposed against brightness, colored light set against gray mists. At dawn the army glows with a purple hue, and "In the eastern sky there was a yellow patch like a rug laid for the feet of the coming sun; and against it, *black and pattern-like*, loomed the gigantic figure of the colonel on a gigantic horse" (pages 24–25). Black is juxtaposed against yellow (page 27), or against red (pages 31 and 149). Smoke wreathes around a square of white light and a path of yellow shade (page 5). Smoke dimly outlines a distance filled with *blue* uniforms, a *green* sward, and a *sapphire* sky (page 250). Further examples of color-contrast, particularly white *versus* black, occur throughout "The Open Boat," and blue is used symbolically in "The Blue Hotel." Crane had an extraordinary predilection for blue, which Hamlin Garland took to be the sign manual of the Impressionists. It seems likely that Crane read Garland's *Crumbling Idols*, but in any case he wrote a novel about an impressionistic painter—the hero of *The Third Violet*. And in one of his sketches he wrote:

> The flash of the impression was like light, and for this instant it illumined all the dark recesses of one's remotest idea of sacrilege, ghastly and wanton. I bring this to you merely as *an effect of mental light and shade*, something done in thought, *similar to that which the French Impressionists do in color*, something meaningless and at the same time overwhelming, crushing, monstrous. (*The Work of Stephen Crane*, vol. IX, p. 246.)

Crane paints in words exactly as the French Impressionists paint in pigments: both use pure colors and contrasts of colors. Dark clouds or dark smoke or masses of mist and vapor are surrounded by a luminous zone; or *conversely*, specks of prismatic color are enclosed by a zone of shade. Shifting gray mists open out before the splendor of the sunrays (page 160). Or *conversely*, billowing smoke is "filled with horizontal flashes" (page 57); "the mist of smoke [is] gashed by the little knives of fire. . ." (page 251). Inside the surrounding darkness the waters of the river appear wine-tinted, and campfires "shining upon the moving masses of troops, brought forth here and there sudden gleams or silver and gold. Upon the other shore a dark and mysterious range of hills was curved against the sky" (page 37; the same scene is duplicated on page 155). Cleared atmospheres, unimpeded vision of perspective, are rarely delineated, and where they occur the precision of vision is equated, symbolically, with revelation or spiritual insight. (One instance of this symbolic use of color appears on page 42.) Dark mists and vapors represent the haze of Henry's unenlightened mind ("He, the enlightened man who looks afar in the dark, had fled because of his superior perceptions and knowledge"). Darkness and smoke serve as symbols of concealment and deception, vapors masking the light of truth. Sunlight and changing colors signify spiritual insight and rebirth (as on page 1). Henry is a color-bearer, but it is not until he recognizes the truth of his self-deception that the youth keeps "the bright colors to the front." In the celebrated impression of the red sun "pasted in the sky like a wafer" Crane is at once an Impressionist painter and a symbolic artist. But more of that later. Meanwhile an important point about Crane's technique deserves mentioning in this brief discussion of Impressionism. The point is that Crane is a master craftsman in creating his illusions of reality by means of a fixed point of view, through a specifically located observer.

> *From their position* as they again faced toward the place of fighting, they could of course comprehend a greater amount of battle than when their visions had been blurred by the hurling smoke of the line. *They could see* dark stretches winding along the land, and on one cleared space there was a row of guns making *gray clouds, which were filled with large flashes of orange-colored flame* (page 198).

Crane presents his pictures from a fixed plane of vision, and his perspectives seem based upon the same principle of contrast as the Impressionists employed:—Darkness pierced by brilliant color (as in the above), or darkness tinged "with a phosphorescent glow."

III

What makes Crane of such exceptional critical interest is the great range and number of comparisons with other artists, echoes and parallelisms which suggest themselves to any critic who has studied the man and his art. The range of cross-references extends from Flaubert and Hawthorne to Mark Twain and Rudyard Kipling, or—in terms of his influence on 20th Century fiction—beyond his contemporaries Frank Norris and Theodore Dreiser to Dos Passos and Hemingway. While Crane's influence can be documented by a formidable catalogue of specific echoes in later American fiction, it persists more significantly in less subtilized form—i.e., his naturalistic outlook in modern novels of slum life, and his concept of the soldier as Everyman in modern novels of war. Maggie's brother (as other critics have pointed out) is a forebear of Studs Lonnigan, and Crane in several of his stories ("An Episode of War" is one example) foremirrors Hemingway.[5] Modern American literature has its beginnings in Mark Twain and Stephen Crane. Crane in his use of dialect and in his stories of childhood links with Twain, Kipling, and Booth Tarkington. Crane's own Tom Sawyer is Jimmie Trescott (in "Making an Orator"), and his *Sullivan County Sketches* and *Whilomville Stories* had their inspirational source in Twain's *Roughing It* and his *Life on the Mississippi* (which was Crane's favorite book). More important is the kinship they establish in the history of American literature: they each brought into fiction new subject matter and furthermore perfected the techniques for manipulating it. Technically, *The Red Badge of Courage* stands in legitimate comparison with *Huckleberry Finn*. They have the same repetitive form, namely repetitions of ironic episodes, and they deal with heroes in quest of selfhood. In *Huckleberry Finn* every episode is built upon the themes of death and deception or betrayal, and the same themes or leitmotivs are central to *The Red Badge*.

The numerous artists who collect or radiate around Crane form, as it were, a literary cartwheel. The spokes which compose it include: the legendary Poe and Robert Louis Stevenson, the adventurer and sketchwriter Robert Cunninghame Graham, the realists Howells and Garland, the naturalists Norris and Dreiser, the impressionists Chekhov and Katherine Mansfield and Conrad and Henry James, and the writers on warfare— Tolstoy, Zola, Ambrose Bierce, J. W. De Forest, Rudyard Kipling, Henri Barbusse, and others. Kipling's war tales and poems paved the way for Crane's *Red Badge* since his soldier-hero, as British reviewers detected, seemed not unrelated to Tommy Atkins. Crane's earliest style was Kiplingesque, as in some of *The Sullivan County Sketches* (e.g., "Killing His Bear"), and something of Kipling's influence infected certain later pieces such as "The Quest for Virtue," "God Rest Ye, Merry Gentlemen," and "Kim Up!"—one of his very last tales. Kipling's subject is similar to Crane's and Conrad's. The key to the whole work of Kipling, as Edmund Wilson defines it, is that "the great celebrant of physical courage should prove in the long run to convey his most moving and convincing effects in describing moral panic." Kipling was one of the three or four influences which Crane admitted, though not always publicly. "If I had kept to my clever Rudyard-Kipling style, the road might have been shorter but, ah, it wouldn't be the true road." Kipling's ballads read to Crane by Irving Bacheller brought forth a burst of excitement. Chance made their careers run similarly too. Both became celebrities while still but youths: Kipling in 1887, when he was twenty-two, and Crane—"a sort of American Kipling" when twenty-four. Both had been journalists before becoming authors, and both wrote about warfare they had never seen. By further coincidence, their greatest recognition came only after their books had reached England, and both suffered their greatest abuse here in America—Kipling, hurt and bewildered, fled from Vermont. Kipling might have expressed the same sad and bitter note that Crane felt, the same lament:

> Now that I have reached the goal—he wrote in a letter from England three years before he died—I suppose that I ought to be contented; but I am not. I was happier in the old days when I was always dreaming of the thing I have now attained. I am disappointed with success, and I am tired of abuse. Over here, happily, they don't treat you as if you were a dog, but give everyone an honest measure of praise or blame. There are no disgusting personalities.[6]

It was Conrad who first identified similitudes between Crane's artistic temperament and his own and who first identified *The Red Badge of Courage*, with its psychological inquiry into the moral problem of conduct, with his own "Nigger of the 'Narcissus.'" (Crane's enthusiasm for this story led him to seek out Conrad in England and thereby become his friend and later his neighbor.) Conrad might have noted further similitudes had he known Crane's "An Experiment in Misery" and *Maggie*, for the short story carries the Conradian theme of Solidarity (the theme also of "The Open Boat") and *Maggie* the Conradian theme of Fidelity—*Maggie* being a study in infidelity or betrayal. Crane and Conrad are closely akin not only in temperament, but in artistic code and in their thematic range and ironic outlook or tone. Both treat the subject of heroism ironically and both contrive for their heroes, usually weak or defeated men, unequal contests against outside forces, pitting them against the sublime obstacles of hostile or indifferent nature. "The Open Boat" epitomizes this subject for Crane, and "Typhoon" does the same for Conrad.

The Red Badge of Courage is readily identifiable with *Lord Jim*, but their differences are, I think, more instructive. Whereas *Lord Jim* has an innate capacity for heroism, Henry Fleming has it thrust upon him by chance and at the wrong moment. For Crane, as "The End of the Battle" testifies, heroism is not a predictable possession but an impersonal gift thrust upon man with ironic consequences. The whole point of his fable "A Mystery of Heroism" is to explode the myth of heroism. The soldier Collins does a heroic deed, but as in Kipling, it's "the heroism of moral fortitude on the edge of a nervous collapse." Collins runs under shellfire to get water at a well and once there he is a hero, "an intruder in the land of fine deeds," but once there the poor hero is cut off (both literally and symbolically) from his fellow men, and the emptiness of his vainglorious triumph is symbolized by the empty bucket from which the wasted water spills as he nervously makes his way back to the men. Crane's characters are always common, insignificant, and virtually nameless persons; no Crane character is heroic, none is a leader, none is an ideal. Crane's concept of man's nature seems rather shallow, his world-view neither penetrating nor magnanimous by comparison with Conrad's.

IV

Every Crane short story worth mentioning is designed upon a single ironic incident, a crucial paradox, or an irony of opposites; all of them are built out of anecdotal material, and all are concerned with the same subject—the moral problem of conduct. Crane's method of construction is similar to the method that Chekhov employs. He constructs his stories by building up to a crucial moment of impasse and collapse. A Crane story consists of that moment when the characters confront the inescapable impasse of their situation, they are caught and boxed in by fate, and then—the moment of spiritual collapse—"nothing happens," and they are left with a sense of loss, insignificance, or defeat, futility or disillusionment.[7] Crane and Chekhov were among the first to eliminate plot.

Crane's best short stories, after "The Open Boat," are "The Bride Comes to Yellow Sky" and three war stories—"A Mystery of Heroism," "An Episode of War," and "The Upturned Face." A slight thing but a perfection, "The Upturned Face" is built upon a paradox. The story is a parable: the ritual of burying a dead man is exposed as a ghastly outrage, more real than riflefire itself. Crane's grotesquerie here is integral to his theme. In "The

Blue Hotel" it is out there on the page, and it is misspent. The story ends with the grotesque image of the corpse of the murdered Swede whose eyes stare "upon a dreadful legend that dwelt atop of the cash-machine: 'This registers the amount of your purchase.'" Here is the legitimate ending of the story. The tone here is at odds with the off-key tone of the appended section, and the theme here is at odds with the trumped-up theme announced in the irrelevant and non-ironic conclusion. "The Blue Hotel" happens to be Hemingway's favorite among Crane's stories, Willa Cather singles it out, and one or another of Crane's critics rate it as "one of the most vivid short stories ever written by an American." But it does not stand up under critical scrutiny. I don't think it needs to be demonstrated that "The Monster," another famous anthology piece which has received undeserved acclaim, is not a unified structural whole. The opinion that "An Experiment in Misery" is "far more important than the more famous and accessible *Red Badge of Courage* or such stories of mere physical accident as 'The Open Boat'" (as Ludwig Lewisohn would have it) can be dismissed without comment.

Crane constructs his stories to effect a single mood, or a series of moods with each unit in the series composed of a contrast. *Maggie*, a sentimental melodrama that borders upon travesty, concludes with the orgy of melodramatic emotion to which Maggie's mother gives vent over the death of the daughter whom she has brutalized and driven into the streets. The final turnabout consists of her last words—a parody of pious sentiment— "Oh, yes, I'll fergive her! I'll fergive her!" The grotesque buffoonery of this mock lamentation is comic enough, but there is grim tragedy in the underlying theme that all is sham, even between mother and daughter. All Crane stories end in irony. Some of them, like *Maggie* and *George's Mother*, end in a minor note—"not with a bang but a whimper." That is the characteristic ending of Chekhov's stories, as one of his critics has pointed out. Crane is a master of the contradictory effect. "The Open Boat," like Chekhov's story "The Kiss," is constructed of alternating moods, each built-up mood of hope or illusion being canceled out by contradictory moods of futility, despair, or disillusionment. This method of the double mood ("qualitative progression," as Kenneth Burke defines it) was Flaubert's major technical discovery. It is the form of *Madame Bovary*, of Joyce's *Portrait of the Artist as a Young Man* and *The Dubliners* (notably "The Dead"), and of almost all of Chekhov's and Katherine Mansfield's short stories. It is the form of Melville's masterpiece "Benito Cereno"[8] and of one of the best pieces Hawthorne wrote—that Kafka-like parable, "My Kinsman, Major Molineaux."

"The Open Boat" and *The Red Badge of Courage* are identical in form, in theme, and even in their configurated patterns of leitmotivs and imagery.

The opening scene of *The Red Badge of Courage* establishes the same hope–despair pattern as the very last image of the book—a golden ray of sun came through the hosts of leaden rain clouds. This sun-through-rain image, which epitomizes the double mood pattern that dominates every tableau in the whole sequence, is a symbol of Henry's moral triumph and it is an ironic commentary upon it. In "The Open Boat" the hope–despair mood of the men is established (and at the same time the point of view prepared for) in the opening sentence—"None of them knew the colour of the sky"—and the final scene repeats the same contrast mood. At the end when the men are tossed upon "the lonely and indifferent shore," the once barbarously abrupt waves now pace "to and fro in the moonlight," and as the sea changes so, we are made to feel, the men change in heart. They experience a tranquillity of mind now, a serenity that is signified by the seemingly quieted waves. But this peacefulness is deceptive, for actually the violence of the angry sea remains unabated. Their victory over nature has cost them one of their brotherhood—the oiler lies face downward in the shallows.

When Crane began writing fiction he began, like Conrad, as a symbolic artist. One of his very earliest stories, "Men in the Storm," is an experiment in symbolism. Yet the greater number of his stories are nonsymbolic. When he does attempt symbolism all too often his potential symbols collapse. The pathetic episode of "An Auction," for one example, intends to be symbolic but remains merely pathetic. In a good number of stories he wastes what he renders, namely realistic details that could readily have been converted to symbolic use. His symbolic technique is best studied in "The Open Boat" and *The Red Badge of Courage*. In "The Open Boat," the very beginning of the story prepares for the final incident, the death of the oiler, by a symbolic detail. The oiler is represented by the thin little oar he steers: "It was a thin little oar and it seemed often ready to snap." In both these works Crane charged every realistic detail with symbolic significance.

Let us examine some of Crane's symbols here and see how they are created. One method of creating symbols is by establishing an oblique correlation (1) between the plight of the characters and their environment (i.e., the landscape or stage-setting—battlefield, sea, or forest), or (2) between the plight of the characters and juxtaposed objects, animals, or other persons whose plight parallels or stands in diametric contrast to the central one. Another method of symbolic transfer is (3) by interrupting the mental action or mood of the character with an external action or object juxtaposed at the correlative or illuminating moment. For example, in *The Red Badge of Courage* the confused mind of the hero is repeatedly objectified in the confused actions of a single object, the recurrent image of the flag. The meaning of the whole book accretes around this dominant or focal symbol.

Symbols are at their most effective when they radiate multiple correspondences, or when they embody different contents (at different times or at the same time). Colors (which Crane used as pattern in early works like *The Sullivan County Sketches*, "An Experiment in Misery," and *Maggie*) become symbolically employed in *The Red Badge of Courage* with the symbolic value of any given color varying according to its location in a specific context. Symbolic patterns of life and death are established by the same color—e.g., the yellow of the sun *and* the yellow uniforms of dead soldiers.

Symbols are generated by parallelisms and repetitions. The chattering fear of a frightened squirrel who flees when Henry Fleming throws a pine cone at him (Chapter VII) parallels the plight or state of feeling of the hero when under shellfire. In "The Open Boat" an implied correlation is created between the confused mind of the men and the confused, irrational and "broken sea." Their mental state is obversely identified with the gruesome and ominous gulls who hover over them, sitting "comfortably in groups" and appearing utterly indifferent to the human plight. Again, the unconcern of the universe is symbolized in the wind-tower which stands before them as they head for the beach:

> This tower was a giant, standing with its back to the plight of the ants. It represented in a degree, to the correspondent, the serenity of nature amid the struggles of the individual—nature in the wind, and nature in the vision of the men. She did not seem cruel to him then, nor beneficient, nor treacherous, nor wise. But she was indifferent, flatly indifferent.

The death of the oiler symbolizes the treachery and indifference of nature, and it is through his death that this truth becomes revealed to them. At the end when they hear "the great sea's voice," they now understand what it says (what life means) because they have suffered. They have suffered the worst that the grim sea can exact from them "they felt that they could *then* be interpreters." Thus the whole moral meaning of the story is focused in the death of the oiler. At the beginning (the very first image of the story), "None of them knew the colour of the sky"; but now they know it. The death of the oiler is foreshadowed and epitomized in the song recited by the correspondent during a moment of childhood reverie. He had known this verse when a child—"A soldier of the Legion lay dying in Algiers"—but then he had never regarded the death of this soldier as important or meaningful. He had never felt any sympathy for this soldier's plight because then he himself had not yet experienced it. "It was less to him than the breaking of a pencil's point." (This image of the pencil point correlates with the opening description of the delicate oar of the oiler, which seemed "often ready to snap.") The soldier's death foretells the oiler's death, the one being an analogy of the other. That Crane stands as an innovator in the technique of fiction is evidenced by his using this structural device of analogy, both in "The Open Boat" and in *The Red Badge of Courage*. It was first exploited by Flaubert, and later by James, Chekhov, and Joyce.

What is important to any artist is that he believe in his themes, not that he experience them. Crane passionately believed in the theme that no man can interpret life without first experiencing it, and he put his belief into actual practice. The result was "The Open Boat." *The Red Badge of Courage*, however, is the product of *imaginative* belief in the same theme. And that fact sums up the paradox of Crane's artistic career. "An Episode of War" contradicts Crane's personal theory. The theme that no man can interpret life without first experiencing it is here inverted. The lieutenant, because he is wounded, sees life with new insight because he is removed from the flux of life and can observe it instead of merely experiencing it. The symbol of his insight is his wound, for it is his being wounded that changes him and enables him "to see many things which as a participant in the fight were unknown to him." Now that he has no part in the battle, which is to say no part in life itself, he knows more of life than others. Life, seen now through this new point of view, appears like something in "a historical painting," or fixed and statue-like. In structure the story is formed of alternations of moods, perspectives of motion and change shifting into picture-postcard impressions where everything is felt as fixed and static. Where we get the point of view of the wounded we get *at the same time* the point of view of the unwounded, and this device of the double vision, which was later employed so expertly by Joyce in "The Dead," Crane first introduced in "The Open Boat." Things viewed by the men at sea are viewed as though they were men on land. This double vision in the point of view manifests the two-part contrast of Crane's theme, sea and land symbolizing two ways of life.

I have said that "The Open Boat" embodies the same theme as *The Red Badge of Courage*—the theme that through suffering, through immersion in experience, men become united, they undergo a change of heart, they come into spiritual insight and regeneration. In change lies salvation. This theme of immersion and regeneration is exploited in *King Lear*; it is uttered by Heyst in Conrad's *Victory*; and it is expressed as the credo of Stein in *Lord Jim*. The way is to immerse oneself in the destructive element. In *King Lear* the destructive element is represented by the storm, in *The Red Badge of Courage* by the battlefield, in "The Open Boat" by the sea. The cynic (the correspondent) becomes the believer. That the men are saved is symbolic of their spiritual salvation.

V

That Crane is incapable of architectonics has been the critical consensus that has prevailed for over half a century: "his work is a mass of fragments"; "he can only string together a series of loosely cohering incidents"; *The Red Badge of Courage* is not constructed. Edward Garnett, the first English critic to appraise Crane's work, aptly pointed out that Crane lacks the great artist's arrangement of complex effects, which is certainly true. We look to Conrad and Henry James for "exquisite grouping of devices"; Crane's figure in the carpet is a much simpler one. What it consists of is the very thing Garnett failed to detect—a schemework of striking contrasts, alternations of contradictory moods. Crane once defined a novel as a "succession of . . . sharply-outlined pictures, which pass before the reader like a panorama, leaving each its definite impression." His own novel, nonetheless, is not simply a succession of pictures. It is a sustained structural whole. Every Crane critic concurs in this mistaken notion that *The Red Badge of Courage* is nothing more than "a series of episodic scenes," but not one critic has yet undertaken an analysis of Crane's work to see *how* the sequence of tableaux is constructed. Critical analysis of Crane's unique art is practically nonexistent. Probably no American author, unless it is Mark Twain, stands today in more imperative need of critical revaluation.

The Red Badge of Courage begins with the army immobilized—with restless men waiting for orders to move—and with Henry, because the army has done nothing, disillusioned by his first days as a recruit. In the first picture we get of Henry, he is lying on his army cot—resting on an idea. Or rather, he is wrestling with the personal problem it poses. The idea is a thirdhand rumor that tomorrow, at last, the army goes into action. When the tall soldier first announced it, he waved a shirt which he had just washed in a muddy brook, waved it in banner-like fashion to summon the men around the flag of his colorful rumor. It was a call to the colors—he shook it out and spread it about for the men to admire. But Jim Conklin's prophecy of hope meets with disbelief. "It's a lie!" shouts the loud soldier. "I don't believe the derned old army's ever going to move." No disciples rally around the red and gold flag of the herald. The skeptical soldiers think the tall soldier is telling just a tall tale; a furious altercation ensues. Meanwhile Henry in his hut engages in a spiritual debate with himself; whether to believe or disbelieve the word of his friend, whom he has known since childhood. It is the gospel truth, but Henry is one of the doubting apostles.

The opening scene thus sets going the structural pattern of the whole book. Hope and faith (paragraphs 1–3) shift to despair or disbelief (47). The counter-movement of opposition begins in paragraph 4, in the small detail of the Negro teamster who stops his dancing, when the men desert him to wrangle over Jim Conklin's rumor. "He sat mournfully down." This image of motion and change (the motion ceasing and the joy turning to gloom) presents the dominant leitmotiv and the form of the whole book in miniature. (Another striking instance of emblematic form occurs in Chapter VI, where Crane pictures a terror-stricken lad who throws down his gun and runs: "A lad whose face had borne an expression of exalted courage, the majesty of he who dares give his life, was, at an instant, smitten abject.") In Chapter I the opening prologue ends in a coda (paragraph 7) with theme and anti-theme here interjoined. It is the picture of the corporal—his uncertainties (whether to repair his house) and his shifting attitudes of trust and distrust (whether the army is going to move) parallel the skeptical outlook of the wrangling men. The same anti-theme of distrust is dramatized in the episode which follows this coda, and every subsequent episode in the sequence is designed similarly by one contrast pattern or another.

Change and motion begin the book. The army, which lies resting upon the hills, is first revealed to us by "the retiring fogs," and as the weather changes so the landscape changes, the brown hills turning into a new green. Now as nature stirs so the army stirs too. Nature and man are in psychic affinity; even the weather changes as though in sympathetic accord with man's plight. In the final scene it is raining but the leaden rain clouds shine with "a golden ray" as though to reflect Henry's own bright serenity, his own tranquillity of mind. But now at the beginning, and throughout the book, Henry's mind is in a "tumult of agony and despair." This psychological tumult began when Henry heard the church bell announce the gospel truth that a great battle had been fought. Noise begins the whole mental melee. The clanging church bell and then the noise of rumors disorder his mind by stirring up legendary visions of heroic selfhood. The noisy world that first colored his mind with myths now clamors to Henry to become absorbed into the solidarity of self-forgetful comradeship, but Henry resists this challenge of the "mysterious fraternity born of the smoke and danger of death," and withdraws again and again from the din of the affray to indulge in self-contemplative moods and magic reveries. The walls of the forest insulate him from the noise of battle. In seeking retreat there to absolve his shame and guilt, Henry, renouncing manhood, is "seeking dark and intricate places." It is as though he were seeking return to the womb. Nature, that "woman with a deep aversion to tragedy," is Mother Nature, and the human equation for the forest is of course Henry's own mother. Henry's flight from the forest-sanctuary represents his momentary rejection of womb-like innocence; periodically he rejects Mother Nature with her sheltering arms and her "religion of peace," and his flight from Mother Nature is symbolic of his initiation into the truth of the world he must measure up to. He is the deceived youth, for death lurks even in the forest-sanctuary. In the pond a gleaming fish is killed by one of the forest creatures, and in the forest Henry meets a rotted corpse, a man whose eyes stare like a dead fish, with ants scurrying over the face. The treachery of this forest retreat, where nothing is as it seems, symbolizes the treachery of ideals—the illusions by which we are all betrayed.

Henry's mind is in constant flux. Henry's self-combat is symbolized by the conflict among the men and between the armies, their altercation being a duplication of his own. Like the regiment that marches and countermarches over the same ground, so Henry's mind traverses the same ideas over and over again. As the cheery-voiced soldier says about the battle, "It's th' most mixed up dern thing I ever see." Mental commotion, confusion, and change are externalized in the "mighty altercation" of men and guns and nature herself. Everything becomes activated, even the dead. That corpse Henry meets on the battlefield, "the *invulnerable* dead man," cannot stay still—he "*forced* a way for himself" through the ranks. And guns throb too, "restless guns." Back and forth the stage-scenery shifts from dreams to "jolted dreams" and grim fact. Henry's illusions collapse, dreams pinpricked by reality.

Throughout the whole book *withdrawals* alternate with *engagements*, with scenes of entanglement and tumult, but the same nightmarish atmosphere of upheaval and disorder pervades both the inner and the outer realms. The paradox is that when Henry becomes activated in the "vast blue demonstration" and is thereby reduced to anonymity he is then most a man, and conversely, when he affects self-dramatizing picture-postcard poses of himself as hero he is then least a man and not at all heroic. He is then innocent as a child. When disengaged from the external tumult, Henry's mind recollects former domestic scenes. Pictures of childhood and nursery imagery of babes recur at almost every interval of withdrawal. Childhood innocence and withdrawal are thus equated. The nursery limerick which the wounded soldiers sing as they retreat from the battlefront is at once a travesty of their own plight and a mockery of Henry's mythical innocence.

> Sing a song 'a vic'try
> A pocketful 'a bullets,
> Five an' twenty dead men
> Baked in a—pie.

Everything goes awry; nothing turns out as Henry had expected. Battles turn out to be "an immense and terrible machine to him" (the awful machinery of his own mind). At his battle task Henry, we are told, "was like a carpenter who has made many boxes, making still another box, only there was furious haste in his movements." Henry, "frustrated by hateful circumstances," pictures himself as boxed in by fate, by the regiment, and by the "iron laws of tradition and law on four sides. He was in a moving box." And furthermore there are those purely theoretical boxes by which he is shut in from reality—his romantic dreams, legendary visions of heroic selfhood, illusions which the vainglorious machinery of his own mind has manufactured.

The youth who had envisioned himself in Homeric poses, the legendary hero of a Greeklike struggle, has his pretty illusion shattered as soon as he announces his enlistment to his mother. "I've knet yeh eight pair of socks, Henry. . . ." His mother is busy peeling potatoes, and, madonna-like, she kneels among the parings. They are the scraps of his romantic dreams. The youthful private imagines armies to be monsters, "redoubtable dragons," but then he sees the real thing—the colonel who strokes his mustache and shouts over his shoulder, "Don't forget that box of cigars!"

The Red Badge of Courage probes a state of mind under the incessant pinpricks and bombardments of life. The theme is that man's salvation lies in change, in spiritual growth. It is only by immersion in the flux of experience that man becomes disciplined and develops in character, conscience, or soul. Potentialities for change are at their greatest in battle—a battle represents life at its most intense flux. Crane's book is not about the combat of armies; it is about the self-combat of a youth who fears and stubbornly resists change, and the actual battle is symbolic of this spiritual warfare against change and growth. To say that the book is a study in fear is as shallow an interpretation as to say that it is a narrative of the Civil War. It is the standard reading of all Crane's writings, the reading of fear into everything he wrote, and for this misleading diagnosis Thomas Beer's biography of 1923 is almost solely responsible.[9] It is this Handbook of Fear that accounts for the neglect of all critics to attempt any other reading. Beer's thesis is that all the works from the first story to the last dissect fear and that *as* they deal exclusively with fear *so* fear was the motivating passion of Crane's life. "That newspaper feller was a nervy man," said the cook of the ill-fated *Commodore*. "*He didn't seem to know what fear was.*" Yet in his art there is fear, little more than that, and in "The Blue Hotel"—so the *Literary History of the United States* tells us—the premonition of the Swede is nothing "but the manifestation of Crane's own intense fear." This equation of Crane's works with his life, however seemingly plausible, is critically fallacious, and the resultant reading is a grossly oversimplified one. Fear is only one of the many passions that comprise *The Red Badge of Courage*; they include not alone fear but rage, elation, and the equally telltale passions of pride and shame. What was Crane afraid of? If Crane was at all afraid, he was afraid of time and change. Throughout Crane's works, as in his life, there is the conflict between ideals and reality.

Our critical concern is with the plight of his hero: Henry Fleming recognizes the necessity for change and development, but he wars against it. The youth develops into the veteran—"*So it came to pass . . . his soul changed.*" Significantly enough, in thus stating what his book is about Crane intones Biblical phrasing.

Spiritual change, *that* is Henry Fleming's red badge. *His red badge is his conscience reborn and purified.* Whereas Jim Conklin's red badge of courage is the literal one, the wound of which he dies, Henry's is the psychological badge, the wound of conscience. Internal wounds are more painful than external ones. It is fitting that Henry should receive a head wound, a bump that jolts him with a severe headache! But what "salve" is there to ease the pain of his internal wound of dishonor? That is Henry's "headache"! It is the ache of his conscience that he has been honored by the regiment he has dishonored. Just as Jim runs into the fields to hide his true wound from Henry, so Henry runs into the fields to hide his false wound, his false badge of courage, from the tattered man who asks him where he is wounded. "It might be inside mostly, an' them plays thunder. Where is it located?" The men, so Henry feels, are perpetually probing his guilt-wound, "ever upraising the ghost of shame on the stick of their curiosity." The unmistakable implication here is of a flag, and the actual flag which Henry carries in battle is the symbol of his conscience. Conscience is also symbolized by the forest, the cathedral-forest where Henry retreats to nurse his guilt-wound and be consoled by the benedictions which nature sympathetically bestows upon him. Here in this forest-chapel there is a churchlike silence as insects "bow their beaks" while Henry bows his head in shame; they make a "devotional pause" while the trees chant a soft hymn to comfort him. But Henry is troubled; he cannot "conciliate the forest." Nor can he conciliate the flag. The flag registers the commotion of his mind, and it registers the restless movements of the nervous regiment—it flutters when the men expect battle. And when the regiment runs from the battle, the flag sinks down "as if dying. Its motion as it fell was a gesture of despair." Henry dishonors the flag not when he flees from battle but when he flees from himself, and he redeems it when he redeems his conscience.

Redemption begins in confession, in absolution—in change of heart. Henry's wounded conscience is not healed until he confesses to himself the truth and opens his eyes to new ways; not until he strips his enemy heart of "the brass and bombast of his earlier gospels," the vainglorious illusions he had fabricated into a cloak of pride and self-vindication; not until he puts on new garments of humility and loving kindness for his fellow-men. Redemption begins in humility—Henry's example is the loud soldier who becomes the humble soldier. The loud soldier admits the folly of his former ways. Henry's spiritual change is a prolonged process, but it is signalized in moments when he loses his soul in the flux of things; *then* he courageously deserts himself instead of his fellow-men; then fearlessly plunging into battle, charging the enemy like "a pagan who defends his religion," he becomes swept up in a delirium of selflessness and feels himself "capable of profound sacrifices." The brave new Henry, "new bearer of the colors," triumphs over the former one. The enemy flag is wrenched from the hands of "the rival color bearer," the symbol of Henry's own other self, and as this rival color bearer dies Henry is reborn.

Henry's regeneration is brought about by the death of Jim Conklin, the friend whom Henry had known since childhood. He goes under various names. He is sometimes called the spectral soldier (his face is a pasty gray) and sometimes the tall soldier (he is taller than all other men), but there are unmistakable hints—in such descriptive details about him as his wound in the side, his torn body and his gory hand, and even in the initials of his name, Jim Conklin—that he is intended to represent Jesus Christ. We are told that there is "a resemblance in him to a devotee of a mad religion," and among his followers the doomed man stirs up "thoughts of a solemn ceremony." When he dies, the heavens signify his death—the red sun bleeds with the passion of his wounds:

The red sun was pasted in the sky like a wafer.

This grotesque image, the most notorious metaphor in American literature, has been much debated and roundly damned by Crane's critics (e.g., Pattee, Quinn, Cargill, and a dozen others) as downright bad writing, a false, melodramatic and nonfunctional figure. Joseph Hergesheimer, Willa Cather, and Conrad admired it, but no one ventured to explain it. The other camp took potshots at it without attempting to understand what it is really all about. It is, in fact, the key to the symbolism of the whole novel, particularly the religious symbolism which radiates outwards from Jim Conklin. Like any image, it has to be related to the structure of meaning in which it functions; when lifted out of its context it is bound to seem artificial and irrelevant or, on the other hand, merely "a superb piece of imagery." I do not think it can be doubted that Crane intended to suggest here the sacrificial death celebrated in communion.

Henry and the tattered soldier consecrate the death of the spectral soldier in "a solemn ceremony." Henry partakes of the sacramental blood and body of Christ, and the process of his spiritual rebirth begins at this moment when the wafer-like sun appears in the sky. It is a symbol of salvation through death. Henry, we are made to feel, recognizes in the lifeless sun his own lifeless conscience, his dead and as yet unregenerated selfhood or conscience, and that is why he blasphemes against it. His moral salvation and triumph are prepared for (1) by this ritual of purification and religious devotion and, at the very start of the book (2), by the ritual of absolution which Jim Conklin performs in the opening scene. It was the tall soldier who first "developed virtues" and showed the boys how to cleanse a flag. The way is to wash it in the muddy river. Only by experiencing life, the muddy river, can the soul be cleansed. In "The Open Boat" it is the black sea, and the whiteness of the waves as they pace to and fro in the moonlight, signifies the spiritual purification which the men win from their contest against the terrible water. The ritual of domestic comforts bestowed upon the saved men by the people on the shore, "all the remedies sacred to their minds," is a shallow thing, devoid of spiritual value. The sea offers the only true remedy, though it costs a "terrible grace." The way is to immerse oneself in the destructive element!

Kurtz, in Conrad's "Heart of Darkness," washed his soul in the Congo, and Marlow, because he had become a part of Kurtz, redeemed the heart of darkness by the same token. Conrad, like Crane, had himself experienced his own theme, but Crane was the first to produce a work based upon it. Crane's influence on Conrad is apparent in *Lord Jim*, which makes use of the same religious symbolism as *The Red Badge of Courage*. When Lord Jim goes to his death, you recall, there is an awful sunset. Conrad's "enormous sun" was suggested by Crane's grotesque symbol and paradox image of the red sun that was pasted wafer-like in the sky when Jim Conklin died. For the other Jim, "The sky over Patusan was blood-red, immense, streaming like an open vein."

Like Flaubert and James and Conrad, Crane is a great stylist. Theme and style in *The Red Badge* and in "The Open Boat" are organically conceived, the theme of change conjoined with the fluid style by which it is evoked. The deliberately disconnected and apparently disordered style is calculated to create confused impressions of change and motion. Fluidity characterizes the whole book. Crane interjects disjointed details, one nonsequitur melting into another. Scenes and objects are felt as blurred, they appear under a haze or vapor or cloud. Yet everything has relationship and is manipulated into contrapuntal patterns of color and cross-references of meaning.

Like Conrad, Crane puts language to poetic uses, which, to define it, is to use language reflexively and to use language symbolically. It is the works which employ this reflexive and symbolic rise of language that constitute what is permanent of Crane.

It is the language of symbol and paradox: the wafer-like sun, in the *Red Badge*; or in "The Open Boat" the paradox of "cold, comfortable sea-water," an image which calls to mind the poetry of W. B. Yeats with its fusion of contradictory emotions. This single image evokes the sensation of the whole experience of the men in the dinghy, but it suggests furthermore another telltale significance, one that is applicable to Stephen Crane. What is readily recognizable in this paradox of "cold, comfortable sea-water" is that irony of opposites which constituted the personality of the man who wrote it. It is the subjective correlative of his own plight. The enigma of the man is symbolized in his enigmatic style.

Notes

*   A portion of "Stephen Crane: A Revaluation" first appeared as the introduction to the Modern Library (College Edition) *The Red Badge of Courage*, by Stephen Crane, copyright 1951 by Random House, Inc. The complete essay appears here for the first time and is used by permission of the author and Random House, Inc.

1.   I wish to thank Miss Josephine La Vecchia and Mr. Sy Kahn for assisting me in the research preparations for this essay. I am also indebted to Miss Roberta Smith, Reference Librarian at the University of Connecticut, for her constant help. This essay was finished prior to the publication of Mr. John Berryman's biography in the "American Men of Letters Series" (*Stephen Crane*, 1950). I have used most of the biographical material listed in *Stephen Crane: A Bibliography*, by Ames W. Williams and Vincent Starrett (1948), and in addition the critical material listed in my forthcoming supplement to the Williams–Starrett bibliography: "Stephen Crane: Critical and Biographical Studies 1900–1952." I have made further Study of Crane's art and achievement in *The Stephen Crane Reader* (Knopf and Heinemann, 1952), a collection of Crane's best works.

2.   See V. S. Pritchett: *The Living Novel*, p. 166. H. T. Webster identified the source of *The Red Badge* as Hinman's *Corporal Si Klegg* in an article in *American Literature* for November, 1939.

3.   From Vincent Starrett's introduction to Williams's *Bibliography*, p. 10. The contrary view is expressed by Ford Madox Ford and by Thomas Beer, who remarks that Crane "was yet a man of letters." In this matter I share Mr. Starrett's judgment.

4. Cited in *Painting in France: 1895–1949*, by G. Di San Lazzaro (1949), p. 28, fnt.

* Page references are to the Modern Library (College Editions) *The Red Badge of Courage*.

5. *A Farewell to Arms* is an inverted *Red Badge of Courage*. Hemingway's hero is the idealistic Henry Fleming now turned cynic, older and already named. Both heroes are virtually without father and without name. Frederic Henry has a given name for a surname, and Henry Fleming has no name until halfway through the book. Through wounds both heroes come into insight and undergo change—but in opposite directions. Crane's progresses upwards toward manhood and moral triumph; Hemingway's descends toward disenchantment, withdrawal, spiritual denegation. In both novels the education of the hero ends as it began; in self-deception. Frederic Henry renounces war, society, the "comforting stench" of comrades, and he makes his "separate peace." But his farewell to arms is as illusory as Henry Fleming's farewell to vain ideals and compromising illusions. Both heroes are deluded: the one believing he can turn his back upon the battle of life, and the other believing he has triumphed in facing up to it shorn of all romantic notions. Both novels are ritualistic, mythic, symbolic, with the dominant symbolism religious.

6. Letter to John N. Hilliard, reprinted from the *New York Times, Supplement*, July 14, 1900, p. 466.

7. Crane's poems have the same structural design and, some of them, even the same plot and mood as his short stories. Paradox shapes them, a single turnabout. "A Youth" is a miniature copy of *The Red Badge of Courage*:

> A youth in apparel that glitterd
> Went to walk in a grim forest.
> There he met an assassin
> Attired all in garb of old days;
> He, scowling through the thickets,
> And dagger poised quivering,
> Rushed upon the youth.
> 'Sir,' said the latter,
> 'I am enchanted, believe me,
> To die thus,
> In this medieval fashion,
> According to the best legends;
> Ah, what joy!'
> Then took he the wound, smiling,
> And died, content.

The would-be assassin of the youth meets an impasse, namely the youth's romantic illusion of wanting to die a happy heroic death in medieval fashion. Similarly in "The Bride Comes to Yellow Sky," the would-be assassin of the newly wed sheriff is disarmed by an ironic reversal of expectations. Contrast likewise shapes the parable poem "I saw a man pursuing the horizon." Henry Fleming is one of several Crane heroes who are men pursuing the horizon. Again, "A man adrift on a slim spar" reproduces the plight of the men in "The Open Boat," and the syllogistic three-line poem in *The Black Riders* (1895) states the germinal situation which developed into the short story, "The Blue Hotel" (1898):

> A man feared that he might find an assassin;
> Another that he might find a victim.
> One was more wise than the other.

8. Mr. Newton Arvin thinks that Melville's "Benito Cereno" has been "unduly celebrated," that the story "is an artistic miscarriage," and that its substance is "weak and disappointing. A greater portentousness of moral meaning is constantly suggested than is ever actually present. Of moral meaning, indeed, there is singularly little." He cannot understand why so much praise has been lavished upon the sinister atmosphere: "it is 'built up' tediously and wastefully through the accumulation of incident upon incident, detail upon detail, as if to overwhelm the dullest-witted and most resistant reader." (*Herman Melville*, pp. 238–40). Mr. Arvin dismisses the whole thing because he can find no large significance in it, but the only way to find it is by insight into the structural principle by which the meaning is formed. Now the fact is that nothing, not a detail or incident, is wasted. Every incident and every detail function to create moods of trust or, conversely, moods of distrust and suspicion. It is not possible to apprehend what the formed meaning or the story is unless it is read in terms of this structural principle of juxtaposed contrasts.

In order to recognize the perfection of a machine it is first of all necessary to recognize the precise purpose and relationship of all its cogs. That much is elementary. Each machine has its own distinguishing kind of form, and one kind must not be mistaken for another. Not subject but form is the primary for establishing affinities between two literary works. In form "Benito Cereno" is identical to *The Red Badge of Courage*. Though differing in intention or over-all theme, they are formed out of similar meanings or subthemes (such as appearance *versus* reality, trust *versus* distrust); episodes in both works are patterned by the motif of deception; etc.

Burke's categories of forms have never before been applied to fiction. They provide the most illuminating key to the nature and form of fiction that I know of. Arvin's *Herman Melville* is, I should add, the best critical study of Melville that has yet appeared.

9. "Let it be stated," says Beer, "that the mistress of this boy's mind was fear. His search in aesthetic was governed by terror as that of tamer men is governed by the desire of women." A very pretty analogy!

10. Henry's plight is identical with the Reverend Dimmesdale's plight in Hawthorne's psychological novel, *The Scarlet Letter*, with which *The Red Badge of Courage* has bondship by the similitude of the theme of redemption through self-confession and, even more strikingly, by the symbol of the forest to signify conscience. The mythology of the scarlet letter is much the same as the mythology of the red badge: each is the emblem of moral guilt and salvation. The red badge is the scarlet letter of dishonor transferred from the bosom of Hester, the social outcast, to the mind of Henry Fleming, the "mental outcast."

JAMES NAGEL

Backgrounds and Definitions: Conrad's "Complete Impressionist"

In early December of 1897, only two months after their first meeting, Joseph Conrad wrote a letter to Stephen Crane expressing his appreciation of "A Man and Some Others" and "The Open Boat," both of which had appeared earlier that year. After voicing his enthusiasm for the two stories, Conrad went on to say that

> you are an everlasting surprise to one. You shock—and the next moment you give the perfect artistic satisfaction. Your method is fascinating. You are a complete impressionist. The illusions of life come out of your hand without a flaw. It is not life—which nobody wants—it is an art—art for which everyone—the abject and the great—hanker—mostly without knowing it.

Four days later, on December 5, 1897, Conrad wrote to Edward Garnett revealing a similar sentiments:

> I had Crane here last Sunday. We talked and smoked half the night. He is strangely hopeless about himself. I like him. The two stories are excellent. Of course, "A Man and Some Others" is the best of the two but the boat thing interested me more. His eye is very individual and his expression satisfies me artistically. He

From *Stephen Crane and Literary Impressionism.* © 1980 The Pennsylvania State University. Reprinted with permission.

certainly is *the* impressionist and his temperament is curiously unique. His thought is concise, connected, never very deep—yet often startling. He is *the only* impressionist and *only* an impressionist.

Conrad was perhaps overly restrictive in suggesting that Crane was "only an impressionist" for, indeed, Crane wrote in a wide variety of styles. Nevertheless, Conrad's assessment apparently impressed Garnett a great deal for a year later, in "Mr. Stephen Crane: An Appreciation," perhaps the most important critical study of Crane's Impressionism published in his lifetime. Garnett himself took the view that Crane "is the chief impressionist of our day."

It is historically important that both Conrad and Garnett regarded Crane, without qualification, as an Impressionistic writer, especially in view of the stature of these two men in English letters of the late nineteenth century. But they were not the earliest of his readers to consider his work in those terms. As early as 1895 reviewers had noted, sometimes obliquely, Impressionistic ideas and techniques in his fiction. Nancy Huston Banks, for example, in reviewing *The Red Badge of Courage* in the *Bookman* in 1895, suggested that the novel "may perhaps be best described as a study in morbid emotions and distorted external impressions. . . . The few scattered bits of description are like stereopticon views, insecurely put on the canvas. And yet there is on the reader's part a distinct recognition of power—misspent perhaps—but still power of an unusual kind." Banks' concern for "impressions" was developed a few months later by George Wyndham in the *New Review*. His essay clarifies the contemporary view of Crane's use of impressions and of their singularity in the fiction of the day:

> Mr. Crane, for his distinction, has hit on a new device, or at least on one which has never been used before with such consistency and effect. In order to show the features of modern war, he takes a subject—a youth with a peculiar temperament capable of exaltation and yet morbidly sensitive. Then he traces the successive impressions made on such a temperament, from minute to minute, during two days of heaving fighting. He stages the drama of war, so to speak, within the mind of one man, and then admits you as to a theatre.

Beyond psychological realism, Wyndham stressed Crane's use of Sensory Imagery to create an immediacy of scene:

The sights flashed indelibly on the retina of the eye; the sounds that after long silences suddenly cypher; the stenches that sicken in after-life at any chance allusion to decay; or, stirred by these, the storms of passions that force yells of defiance out of inanimate clowns; the winds of fear that sweep by night along prostrate ranks, with the acceleration of trains and the noise as of a whole town waking from nightmare with stertorous, indrawn gasps—these colossal facts of the senses and the soul are the only colours in which the very image of war can be painted. Mr. Crane has composed his palette with these colours, and has painted a picture that challenges comparison with the most vivid scenes of Tolstoi's *La Guerre et la Paix* or of Zola's *La Débâcle*.

Crane's imagistic density seems to have impressed Wyndham as being especially effective in creating a sense of "reality" in the novel, for he comments that the book is filled with "sensuous impressions that leap out from the picture" leaving "such indelible traces as are left by the actual experiences of war." Perhaps it was this same sense of realism, born of sensory images, that led Sydney Brooks to conclude in his review that "certainly, if his [Crane's] book were altogether a work of imagination, unbased on personal experience, his realism would he nothing short of a miracle."

The precise nature of Crane's literary "miracle" was difficult for some contemporary reviewers to define, and it eluded many. Rupert Hughes maintained that *The Red Badge* showed Crane to be a slapdash impressionist. John Barrow Allen found it hard to come to grips with and finally concluded that a serio-comic effect seems to he intended throughout." Jeannette L. Gilder, the sister of Richard Watson Gilder, the editor of *Century*, reviewed Crane's war novel for the *New York World* and offered the memorable comment that "at present Mr. Crane is living with a brother at a place called Hartwood, in Sullivan County in this State. He spends a great part of his time out of doors and writes just as little as he can. In this he shows good sense." Perhaps it was thinking of this kind that Crane was responding to when he wrote to Nellie Crouse that "there is only one person in the world who knows less than the average reader. He is the average reviewer. I would already have been a literary corpse, had I ever paid the slightest attention to the reviewers."

But most early reviews were favorable and many alluded to some aspect of Crane's Impressionism, frequently equating Crane's style with devices in painting and photography and even, in one instance, with the phonograph. Harold Frederic, soon to become a close friend of Stephen and Cora, commented in the *New York Times* on Crane's "battle painting" and concluded that "it is [the] effect of a photographic revelation which startles and fascinates one in *The Red Badge of Courage*." Charles Dudley Warner maintained that Crane's attempt in the novel was to "make every page blaze with color, in order to affect the mind through the eye. It is all very interesting. Every page is painted, perhaps I should say saturated, with this intensity of color." Other reviews described Crane's techniques in similar terms. A writer in *Godey's Magazine* described *The Third Violet* as an "impressionistic sketch in dabs of primary color" and another, reviewing *Wounds in the Rain* in the *New York Times* in 1900, saw Crane as an Impressionist who "tries to record, as would a phonograph, not so much action, as the sounds of the small arms and the boom of the big guns." And John D. Barry, commenting on *The Black Riders* in 1901, wrote that "perhaps an explanation may be suggested by the association of Mr. Crane at this period with a group of young American painters, who had brought from France the impressionistic influences, which with him took literary form".

The most significant comments from this period on Crane's Impressionistic techniques appeared in two notable essays: Edward Garnett's "Mr. Stephen Crane: An Appreciation", printed in the *Academy* in December of 1898, and H.G. Wells' "Stephen Crane: From An English Standpoint", which appeared in *The North American Review* in August of 1900, just two months after Crane's death. Garnett argued that "the rare thing about Mr. Crane's art is that he keeps closer to the surface than any living writer, and, like the great portrait-painters, to a great extent makes the surface betray the depths." After enthusiastic praise of *George's Mother*, "The Bride Comes to Yellow Sky," and *The Red Badge of Courage*, he remarked:

> His art does not include the necessity for complex arrangements; his sure instinct tells him never to quit the passing moment of life, to hold fast by simple situations, to reproduce an episodic, fragmentary nature of life in such artistic sequence that it stands in place of the architectural masses and co-ordinated structures of the great artists. He is the chief impressionist of our day as Sterne was the great impressionist, in a different manner, of his day. If he fails in anything he undertakes, it will be through abandoning the style he has invented.

Garnett's perception that life is inherently "episodic" and "fragmentary," and that these qualities inform the structural principles of Impressionistic fiction, constitutes an important step in the critical description of the nature of Crane's art. Garnett clearly regarded an "invention" of Literary

Impressionism by Crane to be a monumental achievement, for he concluded his essay with the comment that "of the young school of American artists Mr. Crane is the genius—the others have their talents."

H. G. Wells echoed both Garnett's praise of Crane's work and his sense that Crane had "invented" a new form of fiction, calling *The Red Badge* "a new thing, in a new school." Wells was also sensitive to the influence of the Impressionistic painters on Crane's fiction:

> For the great influence of the studio on Crane cannot be ignored; in the persistent selection of the essential elements of an impression, in the ruthless exclusion of mere information, in the direct vigor with which the selected points are made, there is Whistler even more than there is Tolstoi in "The Red Badge of Courage."

Wells also praised Crane's use of imagery, especially color imagery in such stories as "The Open Boat," a work Wells regarded as the "crown" of Crane's fiction. Again, however, Wells' emphasis was on artistic control: for him the story had "all the stark power of the earlier stories, with a new element of restraint; the color is as full and strong as ever, fuller and stronger, indeed; but those chromatic splashes that at times deafen and confuse in 'The Red Badge,' those images that astonish rather than enlighten, are disciplined and controlled." In all of this, he saw Crane's work as a radical departure from traditional fiction and as a precursor of a new direction in literature. Crane, Wells concluded, "is the first expression of the opening mind of a new period, or, at least, the early emphatic phase of a new initiative—beginning, as a growing mind must needs begin, with the record of impressions, a record of a vigor and intensity beyond all precedent."

These early reviews and comments on Crane's art are useful in revealing the contemporary understanding of Crane's fiction as Impressionistic and for a sense, stressed especially by Wells and Garnett, that Crane had developed a vibrant new style. But any definition of Literary Impressionism based solely on these reviews would be fragmentary and suggestive at best. Nevertheless, a number of important points were established in these early comments: reality is perceived as fragmentary; fiction that portrays real life will therefore be episodic; artistic control rivaling that of painters is needed to render fiction in this style; controlled patterns of imagery, especially sensory imagery, are essential for recording the impressions of the characters; such methods produce a startling illusion of life, especially in visual terms; and these qualities in Crane's works, handled with artistic skill, point to a new direction in literature. In effect, what these writers saw in Crane's work was remarkably close to what Hamlin Garland predicted as the new wave of literature in his *Crumbling Idols*:

> [T]he novel of the future will be shorter and simpler and less obvious in its method. It will put its lessons into general effect rather than into epigrams. Discussion will be in the relations of its characters, not on quotable lines of paragraphs. Like impressionism in painting, it will subordinate parts to the whole. . . . It will teach . . . by effect; but it will not be by direct expression, but by placing before the reader the facts of life as they stand related to the artist. The relation will not be put into explanatory notes, but will address itself to the perception of the reader.

What Garland in 1894 had predicted for the future, Stephen Crane was already employing in his fiction.

Despite the number of these early essays, and the insights that they provided, nearly a half-century passed before there was any important development in the critical interpretation of Crane's work as Impressionistic. Part of the reason for this delay may well have been the lack of rigor in the critical terminology of the time, in which distinctions among Realism, Naturalism, and Impressionism were not clearly defined. As a result, although there was general agreement about Crane's basic themes and techniques, scholars variously found his work to be representative of all three of these modes and of Symbolism as well. Another variable was the range and complexity of Crane's fiction. Certain critics, looking primarily at *Maggie*, *George's Mother*, and the *Bowery Tales*, concluded with some justification that they closely resembled works of Naturalism. Richard Chase, for example, argued as late as 1960 that "like the other significant new writers of his generation—Frank Norris, Jack London, and Theodore Dreiser—Crane is, generally speaking, of the 'naturalist' school." This view, with some complications, has been widely held, even in recent scholarship. Although Alfred Kazin has proclaimed rather categorically that Crane was a "naturalist by birth," most critics have sensed in Crane's work a number of elements not accounted for in traditional descriptions of either Realism or Naturalism. The result has been a confusion of terms, an uncertainty of critical assertions, and a simplification of the understanding of Crane's work. In *The Poetry of Stephen Crane*, Daniel Hoffman is led to assert that "in technique he [Crane] is comparably varied, essaying impressionism, naturalism, fantasy, realism, and symbolism. . . ." Other equally acute Crane scholars have grappled with the dilemma of a descriptive term for Crane's art, often with less than conclusive results. Joseph Katz, for example, reflected that

> Crane is difficult to label. In his own time he was called either an impressionist or a decadent; but as later criticism sought a perspective on the literary nineties he was variously considered a realist, a naturalist, a symbolist, a parodist, and even a romantic.

Thomas Gullason, in harmony with Katz, maintains that "though he is still called a realist, naturalist, symbolist, impressionist, and existentialist, Crane cannot truly be labelled." What both Katz and Gullason are responding to is, perhaps, the confluence of the diversity of Crane's literary production and the historical application of inconsistent and incomplete definitions of critical terminology.

The record of the scholarship on Crane as an Impressionist provides ample testimony to this problem. Thomas Beer, for example, in his influential *Stephen Crane* (1923), stressed that Crane "was in full flight from the codes of naturalism" and made several references to Impressionistic tendencies in his work, but Beer offered neither a definition of his terms nor a development of his thinking. In contrast, Harry Hartwick. writing in *The Foreground of American Fiction* in 1931, elaborated his views in what is still an important, if often overlooked, discussion of Crane and Impressionism.

Hartwick implies that literary Impressionism derives from painting, specifically from Monet's *Impression, Sunrise* (1872), which presented an image rather than a narrative. He sees the analogous literary manifestation of this mode in the verse of the French Symbolist Mallarmé and in the fiction of Joseph Conrad and Stephen Crane. This type of fiction, he explains, "is a sequence of pictures, visual, aural, olfactory or tactile. . . ." He continues:

> Impressionism is a sensory kodaking, a confused mosaic of details, a rivulet of hyphenated photographs, which the reader himself must fuse into some eventual relationship. . . . Experience becomes a series of "intense moments"; plot loses importance; and from an interest in the larger aspects of his product, the author turns to an interest in "the bright, particular world."

The introduction of scientific objectivity and analysis, he suggests, has its humanistic expression in ethical relativity and the leveling of social rank: "Democracy, impressionism, and relativity in morals are all yoked together, and follow in the track of science." Impressionism violates tradition and suggests

> the collapse of consistency in thought and literature. . . . Experience, it insists, should be broken into fragments, each fragment to be

respected for its own sake, each passing moment or passion to be welcomed individually and squeezed dry before it can escape us.

Hartwick's discussion was a dominant statement of Crane and Impressionism for almost three decades, until Sergio Perosa's study in 1964. During the intervening years, however, occasional comments touched on the subject. For example, in his *Stephen Crane* for the American Men of Letters Series in 1950, John Berryman introduced the subject of Impressionism and quoted a statement Crane supposedly made to a "friend" in New York in 1893: "Impressionism was his faith. Impressionism, he said, was Truth, and no man could be great who was not an impressionist, for greatness consisted in knowing truth. He said that he did not expect to be great himself, but he hoped to get near the truth." Hailing Crane as one of the "few manifest geniuses the country has produced," he nevertheless concludes that Crane is a Naturalist whose work contains Realistic elements at the same time that he states that "Crane was an Impressionist." In a more extended analysis, Charles C. Walcutt, in *American Literary Naturalism: A Divided Stream* (1956), solved the difficulty of clarifying distinctions among movements by simply making Impressionism one of the styles of Naturalism. As a result, he can see Crane's works as an "early and unique flowering of pure naturalism. It is naturalism in a restricted and special sense, and it contains many non-naturalistic elements, but it is nevertheless entirely consistent and coherent." Walcutt's contradictory synthesis is representative of scholarship on this subject. And R. W. Stallman did not clarify matters in his *Stephen Crane: An Omnibus* when he introduced the term "prose pointillism," an interesting but nebulous phrase. Stallman argued that "*Crane's style is prose pointillism*. It is composed of disconnected images, which coalesce like blobs of color in French impressionistic paintings, every word-group having a cross-reference relationship, every seemingly disconnected detail having inter-relationship to the configurated whole." This description has essentially metaphoric reference and does little to clarify the modality of Crane's work, especially since Stallman also contends that "Crane's *Maggie* is par excellence the exemplar of literary naturalism."

But the major documents of the study of Crane's Impressionism to 1970 are four articles by Sergio Perosa, Orm Øverland, Stanley Wertheim, and Rodney O. Rogers which appeared between 1961 and 1969. Perosa's "Stephen Crane fra naturalismo e impressionisnio" explores the thesis that Crane's work presents a "symbiosis" of Naturalistic ideas and Impressionistic methods. He sees the origins of both movements in a common matrix: the development of artistic modes based on scientific principles. As a result, they retained a common bond discernible at the heart of Crane's fiction. Perosa maintains that the major influence on Crane was Hamlin Garland, especially his theory of "Veritism" and his discussion of Impressionistic painting in *Crumbling Idols* (1894). The painters were engaged in an "attempt to apply to traditional painting the new optic discoveries on the nature of colors and on the decomposition and recomposition of light on the means to produce them." Naturalistic fiction, on the other hand, was concerned with the "principles of physiological heredity and social determinism, together with the concept of a scientific, photographic, and documentary reproduction of life, even at its lowest, serve the purpose of social denunciation. . . ." Meanwhile, Literary Impressionism attempts to portray the

> apprehension of life through the play of perceptions, the significant montage of sense impressions, the reproduction of chromatic touches by colorful and precise notations, the reduction of elaborate syntax to the correlation of sentences, which leads to a sketchy, and at the same time evocative, kind of writing.

Having established this theoretical base. Perosa then discusses *Maggie* and the Bowery tales, *The Red Badge*, and, very briefly, a few of the best known stories.

Orm Øverland supplied much of the detail of definition and analysis that Perosa's essay lacked with the publication of "The Impressionism of Stephen Crane: A Study in Style and Technique" in *Americana Norvegica* in 1966. Øverland apparently wrote without knowledge of or benefit from Perosa's earlier work, a persistent circumstance in essays on Crane's Impressionism. Apart from the concern of both scholars for perception in the technique and theme of Impressionistic fiction, Øverland's essay almost directly contradicts Perosa's contentions. Øverland stresses the distinction between Naturalism and Impressionism, especially in underlying philosophy. Naturalists, he contends,

> believed that reality *could* be seized upon while the impressionists went one step further toward "realism" and "objectivity." . . . To the susceptible mind of the impressionist, the surrounding world viewed at large is not simple and well ordered, but an indistinct and obscure picture made up of an irresistible flood of confused and ever changing sense impressions.

Øverland's discussion, broader than Perosa's, ranges throughout the canon providing precise documentation of the elements of style, syntax, and structure that represent Impressionistic techniques. He is especially perceptive in demonstrating Crane's use of fragmented scenes to form episodes, the restriction of narrative comments to perceptions rather than logical conclusions, the use of substitutionary speech, and the unique quality of Crane's imagery. In detailed analysis, Øverland documents examples of Impressionistic methods in Crane's works. However, his essay does not provide a close analysis of an entire work by Crane to demonstrate the full effect of his approach on an understanding of a story or novel.

Stanley Wertheim's "Crane and Garland: The Education of an Impressionist" covers familial biographical matters with a new emphasis. In a few pages, this essay discusses Crane's association with artists, the influence of Hamlin Garland on his literary creed, and the role of Garland's Veritism in *The Red Badge of Courage*. Impressionism, Wertheim contends, has to do with the "subjective rendering of experience," the employment of an "episodic narrative structure," and an emphasis on images of color. Wertheim underscores the importance of Crane's exposure to Garland's lectures at Avon-by-the-Sea in 1891, which Crane covered for the *New York Tribune*. Wertheim maintains that these lectures were not only the source of Crane's Impressionism but also the "starting point of literary impressionism, which stresses the replacing of theoretical knowledge with visual experience as the goal of realistic writing."

Rodney O. Rogers, in his "Stephen Crane and Impressionism," which appeared in *Nineteenth-Century Fiction* in 1969, argues cogently that the link between Impressionistic painting and fiction is not so much a matter of technique, as R. W. Stallman's "prose pointillism" thesis would imply, as a view of the nature of reality. Both painters and writers of the Impressionistic mode base their work on the premise that "Impressionism is a realistic style of description precisely because reality is ephemeral, evanescent, constantly shifting its meaning and hence continually defying precise definition." The effect of this conception on Crane's fiction, Rogers contends, is the creation of a narrative perspective that is distinct from and often even contradictory of the protagonist's sensibility. The modulation of this disharmony in point of view undercuts the stature of the protagonist, displaying his illusions, posings, and naiveté. Hence the manipulation of point of view not only links Crane ideologically to the French Impressionistic painters but also generates the central themes of his fiction.

Taken as a body of work, these essays on Crane's Impressionism, for all their virtues, do not cohere into it unified definition of the mode. Rather, they indicate the need for a more substantial definition of Impressionism as a prelude to a consideration of his work in these terms.

The modern usage of the term "Impressionism" to describe an artistic tendency derives from an exhibition of the *Société anonyme des artistes, peintres, sculpteurs, et graveurs* in the Paris studio of the photographer Nader in 1874. The exhibit contained pieces by thirty artists (among them Cézanne, Degas, Monet, Pissarro, and Renoir), works previously rejected by the conservative selection judges at the Official Salon in Paris. Among the paintings shown was Claude Monet's *Impression, Sunrise*, painted in 1872, a work sometimes credited with giving the name to the movement. In addition, art critic Louis Leroy used the word "impressionist" in his review of the exhibition, and it was quickly adopted as a term of derision. The currency of "Impressionism" to describe this new mode was assured with the formation of an artistic journal entitled *The Impressionist* in 1877.

A good deal of confusion surrounded Impressionism from the first. Emile Zola persisted in referring to these artists and works as Naturalistic, perhaps originating the linking of the two modes still perpetuated in modern scholarship. Renoir resisted the term "Impressionist" because it implied a "school" of painting, and Degas found it difficult to see how the term could be applied to his own work. Conceived in disharmony, nurtured in derision and confusion, and applied without precision, it is understandable that "Impressionism" has had less than clear meaning over the past century. This early lack of clarity contributed to the dissatisfaction of the artists with the movement, and its first wave lasted only until the Eighth Exhibition of 1886, when the term was formally renounced by the artists of the original 1874 exhibition.

Although the terminology of the movement was controversial from the first, a spectrum of ideas and methods gave the group cohesion without the formalized rules of a "school" of art. Its fundamental concept was a rejection of preconceptions about the nature of reality and an attempt to paint what was actually seen, what sensory impressions were available to the individual painter at a given time and place. The concern for immediate impressions required an intense interest in the fluctuations of light and color, with the effect of a more accurate "realism" in the rendering of nature as it is perceived. This position had its intellectual antecedents: Comte, the originator of Positivism, had also distrusted *a priori* assumptions and had stressed the importance of empirical data. A French chemist, Eugène Chevreul, had explored the scientific basis for the modifying influence of juxtaposed colors in *The Principles of Harmony and Contrast of Colors, and Their Application to the Arts* in 1839. And there was a good deal of work in philosophy relevant to Impressionistic ideas, including that by David Hume and the British empirical philosophers on the theory of knowledge, perhaps best represented by Hume's *A Treatise on Human Nature* (1739–10). Despite such influences, however, the Impressionistic movement was not essentially philosophical or scientific; it derived from the minds of artists whose principal concerns were for artistic effect rather than intellectual coherence.

Indeed, as Diego Martelli argued in *Gli Impressionisti*, a pamphlet published in Pisa only six years after the first Impressionist Exhibition,

> Impressionism is not only a revolution in the field of thought, but it is also a physiological revolution of the human eyes. It is a new theory that depends on a different way of perceiving the sensations of light and of expressing the impressions. Nor do the Impressionists fabricate their theories first and then adapt the paintings to them, but on the contrary, as always happens with discoveries, the pictures were born of the unconscious visual phenomenon of men of art who, having studied, afterward produced the reasoning of the philosophers.

And four years before, in 1876, Edmond Duranty had defended the Impressionists in his *La Nouvelle Printure: A propos du groupe d'artistes qui expose dans les Galeries Durand-Ruel* against the charges that their works were mere "sketches and abbreviated summaries." He countered, especially with regard to Degas' work, that

> by means of a back, we want a temperament, an age, a social condition to be revealed; through a pair of hands, we should be able to express a magistrate or a tradesman; by a gesture, a whole series of feelings. . . . *A man opens a door; he enters; that is enough; we see that he has lost his daughter.* Hands that are kept in pockets can be eloquent.

Duranty's remarks are pertinent not only to the painters he was defending but also to the dramatic mode of the writers who were to follow, especially in the role of suggestion, the restriction of expository background information in a scene, and the use of synecdoche.

The variety of concerns represented by the concept "impressionism" is easily suggested by the works and comments of the French painters themselves. Cézanne indicated the "sensational nature of Impressionism, as well as its distinction from Realism, when he declared, "'I have not tried to reproduce Nature: I have represented it. . . . Art should not imitate nature, but should express the sensations aroused by nature.'" On another occasion he wrote to Emile Bernard, "we must render the image of what we see, forgetting everything that existed before this. As Cézanne suggests, visual emphasis is the most striking feature of Impressionistic painting, from the dominant red sun, pasted in the sky like a wafer, shimmering across the bay in Monet's *Impression, Setting Sun*, to the more delicate pastels in his *Sailboats at Argenteuil*. Of particular interest is the obscuring of vision in Impressionistic painting, a systematic limitation of the sensory reception of the essentials of scene. Such obscuring is generally the result of natural phenomena (trees, fog, snow, darkness, distance) or, less often, problems arising from human civilization (smoke, flags, buildings, crowds). So Pissarro, a defender of Neo-Impressionism, will portray a river on a misty and fog-laden morning, as in *L'Ile Lacroix, Rouen*. Claude Monet shows not simply a train depot in *La Gare Saint-Lazare, Paris* but a depot seen through the heavy smoke pouring from the locomotives. In *Boulevard Montmartre, Night*, Pissarro renders the obscured effect of lights along a street in the evening. Distance reduces the background figures in Degas' *Carriage at the Races* to the same kind of "tiny riders on tiny horses" that Henry Fleming perceives across a battlefield in *The Red Badge of Courage*. The effect of distance on vision, especially when viewing human forms, is equally pronounced in Monet's *Vétheuil*.

Another striking dimension of Impressionistic painting that links it to literature of the same mode is the concern for the transience of reality, or more correctly, the ineluctable flux in human perceptions of even the most stale of objects. Monet will present numerous paintings of haystacks from the same perspective at different times and under differing light conditions: the color, the emphasis, the essence of "reality" has changed. He presents the same phenomenon in *Rouen Cathedral in Full Sunlight* and *Rouen Cathedral in Sunlight*; only the light effects have altered, and yet the reality portrayed has changed dramatically. In these and other paintings the fundamental ideology is clear: reality is a matter of perception; it is unstable, ever-changing, elusive, inscrutable.

The implications of this new artistic mode in France were not lost on American intellectuals. As early as 1870, for example, the French opera singer Madame Ambre, in America for engagements with Colonel Mapelson's Italian Opera Company in New York and Boston, brought with her Edouard Manet's *Execution of the Emperor Maximilian*. Four years later the Foreign Exhibition in Boston displayed works by Monet, Manet, Pissarro, Renoir, and Sisley in the first important Impressionistic show in America, although their appearance came at a time when the American public was not quite prepared to receive them. And in 1886 Durand-Ruel came to New York with a large collection of Impressionist paintings which Wells praised with enthusiasm. In this year as well, James F. Sutton of the American Art Association arranged an exhibition in April in New York of over 300 paintings, most of them by Degas, Monet, Manet, Pissarro, and Renoir.

By the late 1880s, Impressionism in painting had been displayed to American society and had become an important topic of discussion and debate. Many Americans, having studied in France, had adopted the mode themselves and were active representatives of the movement. Among the first of these was Theodore Robinson, who returned to the United States in 1888 and displayed his work at the Society of American Artists; later, in 1895, his works were on exhibit at the Macbeth Gallery in New York. Similarly, James Whistler had studied in Paris during the rise of Impressionism and had brought these new ideas back to England and America, as did Mary Cassatt, who encouraged American collectors to buy and show Impressionistic works still scorned by Parisian conservatives. By 1895, in fact, there were enough American Impressionistic painters for John Twatchman and Childe Hassam to form an exhibition of American Impressionists, entitled "Ten American Painters," and to establish with other artists, among whom J. Alden Weir and Willard Metcalf are perhaps the most important, the Academy of American Impressionism.

This activity in painting was familiar to American writers. In 1892, when Stephen Crane was living in the Art Students' League in New York, Cecelia Waern published a brief but important essay, "Some Notes on French Impressionism," in the *Atlantic Monthly*. The thrust of her remarks makes it easy to understand why literary critics of the time would show a certain flexibility in their use of the term "Impressionism" throughout the decade. Waern began with the assertion that

> Impressionism, like most new things, great or small, is at present more discussed than understood. The word itself is elastic, and covers a variety of significations; the teachings of the school, in themselves narrow and definite, are only vaguely known and apprehended even by many professional critics.

Attempting to narrow and clarify the term, she nonetheless concedes that Impressionism sometimes refers to the conception of a work of art and at other times to its technique. Painters, she says, also differ in the degree of clarity they give to objects. But the one thing she sees in all Impressionism is the "visual unity of their picture." Thus, she implies, Impressionism is largely a technique based on optical effect; it is not a school of philosophy. Still, she suggests, there is an underlying idea behind Impressionism: "The great secret of all Impressionism lies in aiming to reproduce, as nearly as possible, the same kind of physical impression on the spectator's eye that was produced on the eye of the artist by the object seen in nature. . . ." Waern's aesthetic of Impressionism in painting embraced principles of form and unity, of the relation of reality to aesthetic production, and of the "effect" of art on the viewer. The literary equivalent of Waern's concept was just beginning to appear in American literature, and it was remarkably close to her definition.

French Impressionist painting attracted the intention of a number of writers who became intimates of the group and apologists for the movement. Emile Zola, for example, had early joined the meetings at the Café Guerbois, which included Monet, Renoir, Pissarro, and, especially important for Zola, Edouard Manet and Paul Cézanne. Other important French writers became involved with the lives and philosophies of these artists, among them the brothers Goncourt, Baudelaire, who became a companion of both Monet and Courbet, Jules Laforgue, who defended the painters in a series of articles, and Mallarmé, whose works show influence from Impressionistic painting and music. In America the literary articulation of the movement in painting came largely through the efforts of Hamlin Garland, who, basing much of his thinking on the work of Eugène Véron, lectured on Impressionism and wrote about it in his *Crumbling Idols: Twelve Essays on Art Dealing Chiefly with Literature, Painting and the Drama*. As is well known, Garland was an acquaintance of Stephen Crane's as early as 1891, and his views indicate the exposure to Impressionistic ideas available to Crane in the formative years of his career.

Garland regarded the fundamental idea of Impressionism as a structural principle: "A picture should be a unified impression. [It] should be the staged and reproduced effect of a single section of the world of color upon the eye." Garland's views are remarkably close to those of Cecelia Waern: that the sensory *effect* of reality, not reality itself, is the subject of such art; that the desire to portray the immediacy of experience excluded basically historical subjects; that the Impressionist aesthetic, although not a formal philosophy, "indicates a radical change in attitude toward the physical universe. It stands for an advance in the perceptive power of the human eye." Garland's literary expression of these concepts he called "Veritism," and, although he was never to fully employ these concepts in his own fiction, his ideas were an important influence throughout the 1890s.

Precisely how much of the discussion of Impressionism in painting and literature Stephen Crane had read or heard is not known, but there is no doubt that he knew painters and painting in the 1890s and that he was particularly aware of Impressionism. From his early childhood, painting had surrounded him. His older sister, Mary Helen Crane, was an artist herself and taught art during the 1880s and 1890s in Asbury Park, New Jersey. As a freshman at Syracuse University Crane had several Impressionistic paintings by Phebe English on the walls of his room. Many of Crane's closest friends and roommates during his early career were painters. Even Cora Taylor, who lived with Crane as his wife, had family ties with painting: "Her father, John Howarth, was a Boston artist, and her great-grandfather, George Howarth, had been an art dealer." Other aspects of Crane's life indicate an almost continuous involvement within painting. In a particularly intriguing episode, R. W. Stallman has recorded that in 1897 Henry Sanford Sennet had brought his young French wife to visit Crane at Ravensbrook. She had known Seurat and spent the evening discussing his work with Crane and Ford Madox Ford. And after Crane's death in 1900, one of Cora's problems was moving all the paintings they had acquired.

The key period in Crane's life for his involvement in painting was his experience in 1892–1893 of living in the Art Students' League with a group of young painters. Here he came to know Frederick Gordon, R. G. Vosburgh, David Ericson, Nelson Greene, W. W. Carroll, Edward S. Hamilton, and Corwin Knapp Linson, who kept a journal of life in the League, and who was both a painter and an illustrator. Before long Crane had been introduced to Henry McBride and Gustave Verbeck as well. During this period, he not only lived and dined with these men but participated in their artistic discussions. As Melvin H. Schoberlin revealed in a letter in 1949, they frequently explored the topic of Impressionism.

Corwin Knapp Linson's record of these years was finally published in 1958. Linson, born in Brooklyn in 1864, had studied in Paris at the Julian Académie and, more importantly, under Léon Gérôme, Lafebvre, and Laurent, at the École des Beaux-Arts, where one of his fellow students was Paul Gauguin. By 1891, when he first met Stephen Crane, Linson was dividing his time between "pure" art and sketches for books and magazines, including *Harper's Weekly* and *Scribner's*, for which he sketched the Olympic Games in Athens. Looking back on this period, Linson acknowledged a uniquely "artistic quality in Crane's fiction: "Had not Stephen Crane been an artist in words he must have used color with a brush." He was especially struck by Crane's use of color to create an "impression" of a scene, particularly in his Cuban sketches. Linson also commented that "Crane's was peculiarly the genius for distilling from a given situation its very essence, fixing it on the page in swift impressionistic sentences tingling at times with a perfect expression, always alive." Indeed, Linson saw the quality of painting in a great deal of Crane's work, even in his description of the Scranton coal region. In return, Crane paid indirect homage to Linson in *The Third Violet*: the painting described as "cows in a wintry barnyard around a central haybox" was by Linson and hung on the wall of his room where Crane used to see it.

There is also evidence from other sources about Crane's awareness of painting and Impressionism. In 1896 Herbert P. Williams, a friend of Crane's and a reporter for the *Boston Herald*, recalled in an interview for the *Illustrated American* that Crane had several Impressionistic landscapes on the wall of his apartment in New York. He added that he believed that these "Impressionistic paintings had been with him since his college days." More recently, Daniel Hoffman has reflected that when Crane was working on the poems for *The Black Riders*, his closest companions were the students of the Art Students' League:

> These young men were studying with the first generation of American art teachers to have brought home the doctrines of Monet, Cézanne, and Seurat. Crane often slept on cots in their studio, and in several stories he drew upon the discussions of artistic theory he overheard—and probably took part in—as well as the difficulties of his artist friends in earning their daily dinners.

And R. W. Stallman recorded in his *Stephen Crane: An Omnibus* that

> Crane knew Albert Pinkham personally; he knew not only Ryder's paintings, but some of Monet's, Winslow's, Homer's, and Frederic Remington's drawings, and he had Brady's poignant photographs to brood over. Coffin's illustrations to Si Klegg, and the apprenticeship paintings of Linson and of Crane's fellow lodgers at the Art Students' League, where he lived during the period when he was composing his own impressionistic paintings: *Maggie* and *The Red Badge*.

Another important study of Crane's relationships with painters during this period is Joseph Kwiat's "Stephen Crane and Painting." Kwiat explores the biographical record of Crane's acquaintance with painters and his use of artists and their work in his fiction. He mentions not only Mary Helen Crane but also Phebe English, an art student with whom Crane became infatuated at Claverack Academy between 1888 and 1890. She gave him some of her paintings and the two remained friends until at least 1892, when Crane became involved with art students in New York.

These studies provide a good deal of information about Crane's involvement with painting, which seems circumambient in his life. These experiences are reflected in his fiction as well. Beyond *The Third Violet*, which has as its protagonist a young painter named Bill Hawker, there are numerous references to painting in general and to Impressionism in particular. Perhaps the most direct comment is in "War Memories," Crane's journalistic recollections from Cuba of the Spanish-American war:

> The interior of the church was too cavelike in its gloom for the eyes of the operating surgeons, so they had had the altar-table carried to the doorway, where there was a bright light. Framed then in the black archway was the altar-table with the figure of a man upon it. He was naked save for a breech-clout, and so close, so clear was the ecclesiastic suggestion, that one's mind leaped to a fantasy that this thin pale figure had just been torn down from a cross. The flash of this impression was like light, and for this instant it illumined all the dark recesses of one's remotest idea of sacrilege, ghastly and wanton. I bring this to you merely as an effect—an effect of mental light and shade, if you like: something done in thought similar to that which the French impressionists do in color; something meaningless and at the same time overwhelming, crushing, monstrous.

Other passages in Crane's works suggest his considerable awareness of art and the artistic world. In "Avon's School by the Sea," for example, he mentions Professor Conrad Diehl, who in 1865 had gone to "Paris and entered Gérôme's atelier classes at the École des Beaux Arts" (VIII, 50–1). Indeed, these remarks about Diehl, as well as those about developments in music, reveal a great deal more cultural sophistication than Crane has generally been thought to possess. Other journalistic essays on similar subjects, including two more articles on art at Avon-by-the-Sea, further suggest his awareness of current controversies in art criticism.

In the first of his war dispatches from Greece, pertinently entitled "An Impression of the 'Concert,'" he reports that "Crete spread high and wide precisely like a painting from that absurd period when the painters each tried to reproduce the universe on one canvas. It merely lacked the boat with a triangular sail and a pie-faced crew occupying the attention in the foreground" (IX, 5). Again, in "Death and the Child," he portrays the reflections of Peza:

> Peza remembered his visit to a certain place of pictures, when he had found himself amid heavenly skies and diabolic midnights— the sunshine beating red upon the desert sands, nude bodies flung to the shore in the green moon-glow, ghastly and starving men clawing at a wall in darkness, a girl at her bath with screened rays falling upon her pearly shoulders, a dance, a funeral, a

review, an execution, all the strength of argus-eyed art; and he had whirled and whirled amid this universe with cries of woe and joy, sin and beauty, piercing his ears until he had been obliged to simply come away (V, 129).

The paintings here described cannot be specifically identified from the brief descriptions given, but several by Degas would work for the dance and for the girl at bath, and Manet's *Execution of the Emperor Maximilian* (1867), which Emilie Ambre had brought on her concert tour of the United States in 1879, could provide a well-known reference for the execution. In brief, references to painting abound in Crane's works, appearing in such unlikely pieces as *George's Mother* and "One Dash—Horses" as well as in the stories involving painters as characters, such as "Great Grief" and "The Silver Pageant."

Unfortunately, there is no statement by Crane to directly link his knowledge of painting with his fictional aesthetic, at least nothing so direct as Ernest Hemingway's comment that he "learned to write looking at paintings at the Luxembourg Museum in Paris." What remarks exist are often reported second-hand and contain frequent contradictions. Some of the most pertinent are in Linson's recollections in his journal.

Linson reports that the first comment he ever heard Crane make about his literary creed was his rejection of sentimentality and his assertion that "a story should be logical in its action and faithful to character. Truth to life itself was the only test, the greatest artists were the simplest, and simple because they were true." This realistic code contained, as Linson remembers, two important qualifications: that the "truth" portrayed would not necessarily be a scientific analysis of reality but rather a "simple fidelity to a man's own vision"; that beyond realism there needed to be an aesthetic element: "His art—of course he must be an artist—could take care of the rest." The one other matter that Linson could recall was Crane's emphatic denunciation of didacticism in any form.

These comments, which Linson recorded in 1892 and 1893, are basically consistent with what Crane said about literature throughout his lifetime. Beyond such brief statements, however, there is no evidence that Crane formulated a precise and coherent theory of his craft to guide him in his writing. As Joseph Conrad later recalled, "we were no critics, I mean temperamentally. Crane was even less of a critic than myself." Nonetheless, the extant record of Crane's principles indicates a general "Realism" qualified by the variable of one's impressions. He could state, on one hand, that one should attempt to portray "life" and at the same time profess, as he did before the "Society of the Philistines" in 1895, that he was a writer "who was trying to do what he could 'since he had recovered from college' with the machinery which had come into his hands—doing it sincerely, if clumsily, and simply setting forth in his own way his own impressions." Crane's indirect confirmation of the accuracy of this statement of his views comes in the fact that he clipped an account of them from a newspaper and sent it to Nellie Crouse.

What is unique about Crane's brand of Realism is his awareness that the apprehension of reality is limited to empirical data interpreted by a single human intelligence. As a result, he can echo William Dean Howells' views of Realism but stress that a novelist should be "true to himself and to things as he sees them." How well he can see them, Crane writes in "The Mexican Lower Classes," is limited: He can be sure of two things, form and color" (VIII, 436). Form and color are as much aesthetic as epistemological, however, and the fact that only they seem verifiable implies severe limitations on an artist's ability to portray life realistically. In Crane's "War Memories," a correspondent named Vernall complains that it is impossible to capture the reality of war in art, to get the "real thing." He explains that this is so "because war is neither magnificent not squalid; it is simply life, and an expression of life can always evade us. We can never tell life, one to another, although sometimes we think we can" (VI, 222).

Crane's understanding of his art, these comments suggest, transcends the purely mimetic functions of slice-of-life Realism in favor of a representation of how things are "seen." But nowhere in Crane's comments are these matters fully developed or made consistent. At times he will assert an affinity with the principles of Howells and Garland, attributing to them an artistic mimesis. In 1895 he asserted: "I decided that the nearer a writer gets to life the greater he becomes as an artist, and most of my prose writings have been toward the goal partially described by that misunderstood and abused word, realism. Tolstoi is the writer I admire most of all." The word "partially" is significant here, especially when taken in the context of Crane's admiration for Ambrose Bierce's story "An Occurrence at Owl Creek Bridge," which is a decidedly Impressionistic story rendering sensory data and fantasy as one, dramatically restricting the sources of information, and stressing confusion over what is real. Crane said that "nothing better exists. . . . That story contains everything." There is some reason for believing, therefore, that Crane's deviations from the norms of Realism were toward a still-developing theory of fiction closely associated with artistic Impressionism.

Thus James B. Colvert reasoned well in "The Origins of Stephen Crane's Literary Creed" in contending that Lars Åhnebrink was short-sighted in viewing Crane's work as simply an extension of French and

Russian Naturalism. Colvert, however, is too limiting in his attribution of Crane's theories of art to the aesthetic credo of Dick Heldar, the protagonist of Rudyard Kipling's *The Light That Failed*, which appeared in serial form in *Lippincott's Magazine* in 1891. Dick Heldar, like Crane's Will Hawker to follow, is an Impressionistic painter who experiments with color, especially with its potential for evoking mood. Despite this similarity to Crane's own work, there is no direct evidence that restricts influences on him to this source; it would be more reasonable to suggest that Kipling's novel was one element in a matrix of concepts that influenced Crane's thinking. Indeed, Kipling's ideas may have reinforced, rather than inspired, Crane's developing aesthetic.

But contrary to the historical assumption that Crane was a reluctant browser into literature, an "untutored genius" who sprang into life fully armed, as Howells would have it, Crane was in fact a serious reader. He had an extensive library and was reasonably conversant in recent literary history. Despite his frequent disavowals of any knowledge of literature, there is evidence that he had read, for example, Anatole France, Henry James, George Moore, Mark Rutherford, Bierce, Hardy, Twain, and Kipling. But his knowledge of literature was a good deal wider than this list and would certainly have included the works of his friends Joseph Conrad, Ford Madox Ford, and Harold Frederic. Of these, James, Moore, Bierce, Conrad, Ford, and Frederic play a role in the development of Literary Impressionism. Indeed, Ford said, some years after Crane's death, that "it was perhaps Crane, of all that school or gang—and not excepting Maupassant—who most observed that canon of Impressionism: 'you must render: never report.' You must never, that is to say, write: 'He saw a man aim a gat at him'; you must put it: 'He saw a steel ring directed at him.'"

Ford's remarks imply a dramatic literature in which direct-sensory experience is rendered without expository intrusion into the flow of sensation. No narrative intelligence asserts the existence of a gun in Ford's passage; the reader must interpret the sensory data himself. This method is at the heart of Impressionism in literature.

As Herbert Muller has observed, Impressionism requires the suppression of traditional concepts subordinating the sensory impulses of actual life in favor of a narrative generalization of that life, some abstraction of its "meaning." The purpose of Impressionistic writing is not polemical, often not even "thematic" in the sense of organizing the details of fiction to point toward a predetermined idea, but rather to render the sensory nature of life itself, especially to make the reader "see" the narrative described. The effect, as Crane's comments often suggest, is to convey to the reader the basic impressions of life than a single human consciousness could receive in a given place during a restricted duration of time. The qualification on the "reality" of these impressions is that they necessarily filter through the intermediate minds of character and narrator and may be subject to distortions from either restricted data or faulty interpretation of it. In effect, the impressions may be rendered with meticulous fidelity; or they may not; the reader is forced to exercise a continuous skepticism about the reliability of narrative assertions of judgment and of fact.

Fiction thus presented implies a philosophic base, one well described by Paul Ilie:

> The assumption is . . . that the immediate is in an incessant state of rapid flux, with an infinite number of sensory phenomena occuring in as many moments in the time continuum. Ultimate reality, however, belongs to the realm of human consciousness, whose instruments for monitoring those phenomena are the sensory faculties, through the medium of sensation. Impressionism, consequently, is the technique by which one moment of reality is comprehended after the sensation has been modulated by consciousness and arrested in time.

Given a slightly different formulation by Page Stegner, the philosophy of Impressionism

> establishes reality entirely in the stream of sensations. Fundamentally, impressionism is a statement of the subjectivity of reality and the variety of human responses to . . . experience. Memory, imagination, and emotion guide the mind in its ordering of individual consciousness and become the basis for artistic representation of experience.

Implicit in art based on the confluence of sensation with secondary interpretation is a necessary distinction between reality as perceived and reality itself. The two may be harmonious, an assumption central to Realism, but more often there is discord caused by factors within reality that distort its sensory signals (distance, fog, obscure sounds, darkness, obstructions) or within the receiving interpretive intelligence (fears, dreams, fantasy, preoccupations). The logic of Realism depends on a consistent reliability of both interpretation and perception; the logic of Impressionism suggests that this correspondence is never certain and that the inscrutability and flux of life are its fundamental reality. Impressionistic fiction involves the constant interplay between experience and comprehension, the "apprehension of life through the play of perception," qualified by the constant awareness that any description or presentation of reality is dependent upon the clarity with which it is perceived.

Depending upon emphasis, an Impressionistic writer can modulate his fiction between the "objective" stance of presenting sensations at the instant of reception, and before cognitive processes have begun to interpret and formulate them into patterns of meaning, and the "subjective" stance of recording the internalization of sensory experience, what a given mind understands having received and analyzed the data. An extension of objective Impressionism would lead to a photographic Realism, one with a high order of fidelity to the external world. An extension of subjective Impressionism would lead to an emphasis on the internal world, to psychological Realism, and to stream-of-consciousness in narrative technique. In practice, Impressionistic fiction tends to blend these possibilities.

Fiction based upon these concepts necessarily creates difficulties in the generation of themes, for empirical sensation does not organize itself around consistent ideas and often stops short of thematic or teleological implications. However, in both its central premise and narrative modalities, Impressionism suggests that "reality is empirical, evanescent, constantly shifting its meaning and hence continually defying precise definition." As a result, the characters in Impressionistic fiction are constantly in a state of having to interpret the world around them and to distinguish the "real" from their own views of it.

The truth-illusion in Impressionism has been perceptively defined by H. Peter Stowell in his discussion of Chekhov as an Impressionist who presents characters who "perceive only the limited ambiguous, and ultimately unknowable surfaces of a reality of the senses." The thematic center of such fiction concerns itself with a character's ability to understand reality, most often presented in terms of the metaphor of vision: a character's ability to "see" becomes synonymous with his ability to interpret experience correctly. Comprehension is presented in narrative terms as apprehension. A character might persist throughout a work in being unable to perceive reality accurately, thus living in a world of illusions and blindness. He might receive restricted, disordered, or ambiguous signals from the external world and be limited to perpetually tentative judgments. He may also reason quite logically from unreliable and incomplete data and arrive at an inaccurate formulation. At best, he might accumulate bits of data that ultimately coalesce into a unified generalization consistent with the sensations he has received, at which point he experiences a sudden moment of insight in a Joycean "epiphany."

Beyond the central truth-illusion theme, a number of important subordinate themes appear in Impressionistic fiction. One of these is the isolation that results from the individualistic nature of empirical limitations. Basically, in Impressionism, each character lives alone, alienated from other characters, uncertain of reality. If a character is forced to an ethical choice, his awareness of the limitations of his knowledge forces him to a point of crisis and despair. As Marston LaFrance explains the concept,

> morality must be the creation of man's weak mental machinery alone; but even the best of men, the most personally honest, is prone to error and thus liable to bring misery upon himself and others because the mental machinery often distorts that reality which he must perceive correctly if his personal honesty is to result in morally significant commitment.

To state it briefly, Impressionism is focused on the central truth-illusion theme, modulated by differences in individual abilities to perceive reality and to interpret it.

A fictive mode that presents such themes must render its reality in an aesthetically compatible form, in a manner which itself suggests a restriction of knowledge and shifting, uncertain views of the world. Impressionistic writers have experienced with nearly every dimension of standard fiction, creating dramatic and ironic modes of narration, plots that violated chronology, and narrative lines that are associative, retrospective, or discontinuous. Life, as joseph Conrad and Ford Madox Ford stressed on several occasions, presents a series of disjointed sensory experiences. Fiction that shows life must be evocative and dramatic, limiting exposition and authorial intrusion, and presenting the sensory life of a character. The narrator evokes these sensations in a highly controlled style which seeks *le mot juste* and *l'épithète rare*, presenting a scene in the fewest possible words: "Lightning is a match struck against the sky and the sun is a red wafer." The focus is on episodes of isolated activity rather than lengthy patterns of coordinated events; characters are developed dramatically rather than through expository description; the emphasis is on the minds and actions of all characters rather than on the interpretive analysis of the narrator.

The crux of these devices is the method of narration, the central concern of Impressionistic literature. The basic concept was aptly stated by Ford: "[W]e saw that life did not narrate, but made impressions on our brains. We in turn, if we wished to produce on you an effect of life, must not narrate but render. . . ." The point of rendering life rather than narrating it, of showing rather than telling, relates to the realization that "to hear an event is more immediate than is hearing about an event." It is a sense of immediacy, the process of perception, which gives Impressionism its unique quality and which leads to its coordinate devices. Sensory perception necessarily implies a receiving intelligence; the identity of that intelligence can vary according to a variety of patterns within the Impressionistic mode. One stratagem that is inconsistent with the idea and themes of Impressionism, however, is the presence of the author in fiction. The perceiving intellect must seem to be that of the character, a fictive personality serving as narrator, or a number of characters who see reality in different terms.

In general, Impressionistic fiction is not often written in traditional first person because the standard first-person narrative does not describe the immediacy of experience; he is recapitulating rather than experiencing, using memory rather than sensation. First-person narratives enjoy spatial immediacy but temporal dislocation. There is customarily a double time: the time of the action presented from the time of the telling. This distance creates a sense of remoteness from the experience itself, one difficult to render Impressionistically. First person is, however, reconcilable with Impressionistic ideas in a number of ways: the dichotomous times of telling and action can be presented as a dramatic "present" time. This device demands a suspension of disbelief in that the reader must be convinced that the sensations described are being recorded the instant they occur by a person who is acting and not writing. Another alternative is the juxtaposition of two or more narrators describing the same pattern of events so that the concern is on the way in which their minds differ in perceiving reality. But both of these are relatively sophisticated devices that were not common in Impressionism until the twentieth century. A third narrative mode of Impressionistic first person is the complex device of uncertain or unreliable narration, in which the narrator searches for the truth of his own experience, for the meaning of what has happened, for implications unrealized at the time of action. These variations, however, do not play an important role in the fiction of Stephen Crane.

A similar problem exists with the use of an omniscient narrator: for the basic implications of omniscience are irreconcilable with the notion of a limited view of reality and of the relativity of empirical data. As a result, omniscience is not common in Impressionism, although it can play a role if its function is not to state the truth, not to intrude with evaluation or comment, not to provide background information for its own sake, but rather to qualify the consciousness with which the dominant narrative mind is identified or to provide a context for its activity. To be consistent with Impressionism, such comments could describe the conditions that cause the other narrators or characters to perceive experience in a certain way or provide a point of contrast, a superior perspective from which the characters' thoughts become ironic. Omniscience used in this way implies not so much comprehensive knowledge as the diminished reliability of an alternative narrative consciousness.

The norm in Impressionistic narrative devices, however, is the creation of a narrative intelligence that is as restricted in interpretive power as any of the characters. As a result, narrative assertions beyond scenic descriptions are limited to sensational experience, reflective moments, and musings that carry no guarantee of authenticity beyond their occurrence as thought. The constant unreliability of this mode lends itself to two basic modulations: the possible inaccuracy of narrative assertions, whether sensory or interpretive, can be explicitly acknowledged in statements of uncertainty, qualifications that the data "seems" to suggest a given conclusion or that an event "must have" taken place. This device is generally reserved for occasions in which the character has difficulty perceiving an event, is not present, or in some other way is denied access to primary impressions. The other tendency, to report data as though there were no qualifications on its reliability, creates a subtle irony when the reader recognizes that the assertions are not necessarily true, especially when they involve some degree of evaluative judgment.

This device generally takes the form of the identification of the narrative intelligence with the mind of the protagonist, rendering his sense impressions, judgments, memories as though all were fact. The character becomes the center of intelligence, replacing author and narrator, and as the narrator–character distinction diminishes so does the distinction between illusion and reality. As a result, the reader has no access to data outside of the sensory awareness of the protagonist, no reliable information against which to measure the judgment of the narrator other than the narrator's revelations themselves. The reader is forced to the uncomfortable realization that the

> impression of the perceiving mind is quite distinct from the phenomenon stimulating the impression, and although impressions may be the only source of human knowledge, the perceiving intelligence in recognizing the stimulus apprehends it in terms formulated by the mind itself.

The result is a persistent unreliability of narrative stance similar to what Robert Browning presented in the form of the dramatic monologue. The reader cannot supersede the epistemological level of the center of intelligence and thus receives fragmented and potentially unreliable information which is often distorted and ambiguous.

Even within this realization a distinction may be drawn between the objective and subjective modes. In the objective method, the fictive data derives from the primary level of sensory reception, before cognitive processes have analyzed and organized it into comprehensive patterns. There is a high degree of reliability that the data received reflects the world the character experiences. Such narrators function as "acceptors" of life, presenting experience with little reflection or comment. The narrator's role is objective in all but one sense: impressions are rendered in terms of language. Verbal evocation implies some degree of understanding, memory, and conceptualization on the basis of existing categories of knowledge. Even the simplest sensory experience undergoes some evaluation and reconstruction to be formulated in words. This process represents the irreducible medium of expression, one which has its corollary in all forms of art. To represent life in art, some conceptual activity, whether associative or discriminatory, is inescapable. With this qualification in mind, the mode of rendering primary perception can be regarded as the "objective" pole on a continuum of narrative methods.

The "subjective" pole presents impressions after the data has been received and filtered through the narrator's mind. In the process, the reliability of the data diminishes in that the additional level of mental activity adds a "subjective valuation superimposed upon sensory objectivization." As Paul Ilie has indicated, in this method "concomitant feelings [are] evoked at the same time that the sensorial impressions are being registered, or else they are sentiments that arise in response to the stimulation of those sensations." The subjective valuation represents the judgment of the narrator and possesses only a tentative validity; it does, however, reveal important information about the character who forms the center of intelligence, revealing his emotions, sapience, illusions, sensitivity, prejudices. This is especially true when the subjective judgment is at odds with the objective impressions. In these cases the first can be measured against the second to provide a qualitative expression of a character's comprehension of the world.

Another variation of Impressionistic narration is the device of "parallax," the method of presenting a scene as perceived by multiple narrators. There are many possibilities for the identity of the two or more narrators: an unidentified narrator may be contrasted to a character acting as a center of intelligence, or characters may be contrasted to each other, both resulting in a narrative irony that juxtaposes views. A work rendered through parallax develops a conflict in the mere statement of what is real, making it an expression of the very concept of Impressionistic thought. In all forms, however, Impressionistic narrative methods are related to the conception of life as apprehensible only through empirical data: any narrative judgments are necessarily restricted and potentially unreliable. Whether the method of presentation is objective or subjective, whether it presents parallax or stream of consciousness, the central concern implied by the method itself is epistemological and relates the methodology of the fiction to its thematic content.

The central theme and basic narrative methods of Impressionism also have some influence on the types of characters portrayed and on the way they are pictured. For example, since the protagonists often serve as centers of intelligence, as the receptors of sensory experience, they must be mobile and percipient to provide a wide range of sensory awareness. If they are treated ironically, as blind to experience, incapable of new realizations, they have an antipathetic relationship to a more sensitive reader. But most often, Impressionistic characters are organic, ceaselessly in the process of becoming themselves, as Maria Kronegger states it. Characters who are in the process of forming their understanding of reality are capable of experiencing an epiphany, the central plot development for most Impressionistic fiction.

Impressionistic characters are presented dramatically. Since, with the exception of centers of intelligence, there is no narrative capacity to enter their minds or to explore their backgrounds, what is known about them must change from what they do, from what they say, and from what other characters say about them. If the narrative voice is identified with the mind of the protagonist, as is often the case, there is access to one fictive mind and the capacity for direct psychological depth in one character. Since this is a severe limitation in comparison to various omniscient modes, Impressionistic fiction has a tendency to seem shallow, to present the surface of character and action without the depth of narrative analysis.

This sense of shallowness takes several forms. For one thing, the names of characters have no means of introduction until they are mentioned in the dialogue or until the narrator has some reason to think of them in terms of names. As a result, characters are often known by descriptive epithets developed from their most observable characteristics. A character will be labeled the "cowboy" if he is the only such in a group, or the lieutenant if his rank distinguishes him among soldiers, or the "little man" if he is smaller than his compatriots, or the "oiler" if his occupation is his primary distinction. Under some conditions, at night or in a fog, characters may be referred to simply as "figures" or "forms," since sensory data provides no means of determining that they are human beings. Once a character is identified, however, once he is seen clearly or his name is spoken, his name and specific identification become part of the knowledge of the narrator and serve from that point onward as the reference to the character.

The narrative methods of Impressionism also have an impact on the employment of figurative devices. Since the source of data is restricted to the interaction of a limited intelligence with the phenomenological world, the empirical nature of that experience is rendered in images. Indeed, since reality is largely sensory, the images that formulate sensation are the basic unit of narration. Human experience is not projected as an organized continuum of thought and action but rather as a series of images in sequence which may or may not suggest a coherent whole. As Orm Øverland has postulated:

> Seeking an expression for an ever changing and transitory appearance, the impressionist's images naturally tend to be particular and personal rather than general and universal. They do not profess to reveal about the objects or situations described any deep and hidden truth which will be valid for all time. The aim is merely to convey the immediate impression evoked by a certain set of circumstances, the interplay of which would most probably occur only on that one and unique occasion.

This reasoning further implies that an Impressionistic writer would tend not to use symbols in fiction, for symbolism requires an abstract and consistent frame of reference that provides extensional meaning for the literal vehicle. The use of a dominant symbol, as is common in Naturalism, implies a more reliable and organized view of reality than would be consistent with the philosophy of Impressionism. Such referential associations as suggest themselves from context might accrue to an image; organic metaphor is possible; but symbolization, by virtue of its referential method, is rare and potentially inconsistent with the assumptions of Impressionism.

The imagery used in Impressionism is related to its source in the narrative consciousness. If the narrative method is objective, limited to sensory evocations of scene and action, the images tend to be descriptive, verbal equivalents of experience. Although all of the senses may be involved, the dominant sensory images are visual and involve various modifications of sight: light, shadow, color, form, depth. The imagery is suggestive rather than definitive, recording brief sensations without organization and interpretation (the glint of the sun on a rifle, for example) sometimes without indications of understanding. It is this mode of imagist evocation that most clearly resembles the effects of Impressionist painting, and it may have been this effect that R. W. Stallman had in mind in using the phrase *prose pointillism*.

The subjective tendency of narrative method, in which narrative data derive from the mind of the narrator after interpretation has begun, allows for greater variation in the nature of imagistic expressions. The imagery suggests not only sensory experience but how it is perceived and understood. The objective description of war would present images of the sights and sounds and smells of the scene; the subjective image of war might translate the enemy soldiers into monsters if the protagonist's mind perceives them as such. In the subjective mode, the images derive their significance not from the external world but from what they suggest about the mind of the character. The subjective imagery of Impressionism tends toward Expressionism; the more general handling of figurative devices in Impressionism resembles Imagism and recalls T. F. Hulme's contention that images were the "real substance of experience" and Ezra Pound's idea that an image is a device "which presents an intellectual and emotional complex in an instant of time." But basically, Impressionistic imagery presents the verbal equivalents of sensory experience and the subjective values of that experience as formulated by the mind of the protagonist.

The employment of plot and structure in Impressionism also derives from the implications of the narrative method. The writer is faced from the beginning with the problem of creating a coherent work of art based on the fragmentary episodes the protagonist experiences. Since human life is composed of the "movement of discontinuous momentary fragments," fiction that attempts to reproduce life must render it in terms of brief episodes, abbreviated narrative units that cover a single experience in the center of intelligence. If the narrative method is largely objective, the episodic units are likely to be discrete and equated to one another only by the continuity of scene and character. Sometimes, however, the episodes lead to a cumulative significance which the character experiences as epiphany.

Episodic structure also lends itself to narrative parallax and the juxtaposition of scenes from various points of view. A related device is time shift; since episodes do not imply a continuum of activity, they may be presented in virtually any order, even in violation of chronology. Each episode is basically a time shift unexplained by expository comment and determinable largely through internal data, the movement of the sun, people, or other events that require time to occur. In the subjective mode of narration, however, there is room for the associative arrangement of episodes as the interplay between experience and memory relates scenes to one another. The principle of organization by psychological time, by thematic association which selects the episodes to be presented and gives them a developmental order, creates the potential for a structural unity in Impressionism despite its focus on isolated impressions. As Hamlin Garland suggested about painting, even isolated episodes may be arranged to give the whole of a work a satisfying artistic order, a sense of design that transcends the limitations of episodic structure.

As a total aesthetic, the themes and techniques of Impressionistic fiction derive their coherence from the assumption that human life consists of the interaction of an individual intelligence with a world apprehensible only in terms of sensory experience. The narrative methods may present the objective experience of the reception of sensation, or the subjective interpretation of sensation, or two or more modes in narrative counterpoint. The characters, especially protagonists, are in a continuous state of flux, never fully comprehending themselves or the world around them, never able to grasp a generalization that explains life to them. They are subject to uncertainty and delusion, to diminution of stature, to ironic and satiric treatment, but they are also capable of percipient states in which they realize something new about their lives. The figurative devices tend to be sensory images that serve as the correlatives of empirical data and derive their meaning from context; since there is no stable referential schema, there are few symbols. The narration proceeds by means of fragmentary episodes of discontinuous awareness which achieve unity through continuity of scene or character, juxtaposition, association, or theme. The result in a total work is a fiction that resembles the sensory nature of human experience, no more necessarily teleological than life itself, and no less dramatic and meaningful.

This brief postulation of the aesthetic of Literary Impressionism is theoretical, and no single work is consistent with this model in all respects. Nevertheless, even a tentative description of a literary mode is helpful in distinguishing among tendencies within a work and for making discriminations among modes within an historical period. Realism, Naturalism, and Impressionism, being nearly concurrent historically, share many characteristics: natural settings, an anti-Romanticism that eschews mystification, and concern for the hard life of common Americans. But there are also distinctions among them, differences obscured by a general confusion in terms. Lars Åhnebrink's comment in *The Beginnings of Naturalism in American Fiction* indicates the depth of the problem:

> During the nineties and even after, the discussion of literary theories was confusing because of the looseness of terms used. In general, in the eighties and nineties the movement usually called naturalism went under the name of realism. . . .

Åhnebrink's sense that the terms of the period lacked rigor is unassailable, but perhaps some disorder is inevitable when a disparate group of scholars employ ill-defined verbal indicators to a diverse body of work. Another problem is that critics rarely discuss the same aspects of art when they speak of a movement. Some regard a movement as basically historical, others as the expression of philosophical principles, still others as artistic categories, and some as sociological developments. In addition, many, Crane among them, experimented with several modes and rarely wrote anything with complete fidelity to one school. Nevertheless, recognizing that a definition of a literary mode describes tendencies rather than absolutes, it is essential to provide some indicators for distinguishing Impressionism from Realism and Naturalism.

Many aspects of Naturalism are distinct from those of Impressionism, especially in narrative method, imagery, and theme. If Impressionism derives its themes and techniques from the premise that reality is apprehensible only through empirical experience, Naturalism develops from the concept of determinism. The specific deterministic agent in Naturalism varies from genetic to environmental, but in either form it is usually pessimistic. Heredity functions not only to instill personality traits in the characters but also to link primitive, animalistic origins of human life, to a time when irrational feelings dominated cognitive abilities. The environmental forces in Naturalism are generally socioeconomic, resulting in a tendency to depict lower-class characters struggling for survival in an alien and often hostile society. As Åhnebrink summarizes these ideas,

> *Naturalism* . . . is a manner and method of composition in which the author portrays *life as it is in accordance with the philosophic theory of determinism* (exemplified in Zola's *L'Assommoir*). In contrast to a realist, a naturalist believes that man is fundamentally an animal without free will. To a naturalist man can be explained in terms of the forces, usually heredity and environment, which operate upon him.

The artistic techniques of Naturalism derive from these ideas. The portrayal of forces beyond the control and comprehension of individual characters cannot easily be rendered in terms of the activity of their minds. As a result, the tendency in Naturalism is for an omniscient narrative consciousness which tells rather than shows its story and which provides voluminous expository data about the characters and events. Naturalistic fiction is often "accumulative and ponderous," scientifically analyzing the forces that drive the characters toward their destinies. Since determinism precludes individual choice, the ethical behavior of the characters is not a prime concern, nor is their individualism, for they function largely as representatives of social and economic groups. All of this is in direct contrast to Impressionism, in which reality is established through an individual's view of it and which restricts narrative data to the mind of a character. Naturalism also allows for greater implementation of characters who remain static for the entire work. Indeed, since they are frequently victims of external forces, they are often grotesques, or derelicts from the lower class, or compulsive monomaniacs.

Since the philosophy of Naturalism implies a stable conception of reality in which influences can be analyzed and documented, it is possible to use this frame of reference as a basis for symbolization. Symbolism depends upon stable abstractions for its extensional meaning; in Naturalism those abstractions are suggested through symbols of animalism, depravity, lust, or greed, when the referent is a genetic force, or the jungle, or machinery, or primitive humanity when describing the environment. Often the imagery of Naturalism, rather than its themes, reveals its Darwinian influences. Plot development in Naturalism tends to portray a history of causality for human tragedy; the figurative devices suggest the specific agents that impel the plot.

Although all of these characteristics are rarely found in precisely this form in any single work of fiction, a story such as Frank Norris' "A Deal in Wheat" can serve as an example of the mode. The protagonist is a simple, well-intentioned farmer who struggles hopelessly against economic forces beyond his control. The omniscient point of view is essential for revealing the economic system that ruins him; his particular case is emblematic of the ills of unchecked capitalistic power; the plot contrasts his hopeless plight against the barons of industry and reveals the inevitable human tragedy that results from their competition; and the tone of pessimism underscores the deterministic themes.

If the relationship between Naturalism and Impressionism is one of ideological and artistic antithesis, the distinctions between Impressionism and Realism are much more subtle. W. W. Sichel, writing in the *Quarterly Review* in 1897, maintained that "what is vulgarly known as 'Realism' has indeed nothing necessarily in common with impressionism at all." Unfortunately, Sichel's concept of Impressionism was based on the artist's need to "recall an emotion," an indicator so nonrestrictive that he could discuss Donne, Sterne, and Keats as Impressionists. More recently, Jacob Kolb has discussed the difficulties of using Realism with precision:

> The term "realism" has had a remarkable vogue, although its popularity seems to be inversely proportional to the precision with which it has been used. It is a term which is in great need of clear definition, not only because of its constant general and critical use, but also because of the importance to literary study of the concepts which the term implies.

The sorts of nonrestricative indicators that Kolb complains about are present in Åhnebrink's definition: "*Realism* is a manner and method of composition by which the author describes *normal, average life* in an accurate and truthful way (exemplified in Howells' *The Rise of Silas Lapham*)." Although Howells' novel may well be a model of Realism, the more general attribution of mimesis to Realism ignores the fact that Realism, Impressionism, and Naturalism are all essentially mimetic, although they may differ in their assumptions about reality. And of course this definition indicates nothing of the fictional methods employed to present a mimetic portrait.

In basic philosophy, Realism seems to differ from Impressionism in holding three coordinate postulations:

1) that there is a real world (independent of man's knowledge)
2) that it is possible to know this world, and
3) that it is possible to write about it accurately in fiction.

The difficulty of determining that the "real world" consists of is solved in principle by invoking what Edwin Cady calls the "theory of common vision" and by attempts to "approximate the norm of experience." As a result, Realism embraces an essentially "Benthamite doctrine that the most war is that which is experienced by the greatest number." At a meeting of the Modern Language Association in 1967, six essential characteristics of Realism were isolated: "fidelity to actuality, objectivity (or neutrality—the absence of authorial judgment), democratic focus (particularized ordinary characters), social awareness (and critical appraisal), reportorial detail, and colloquial expression." If the "fidelity to actuality" picture creates certain philosophical difficulties, it is nevertheless useful in reaffirming that Realism presumes to describe locality and that, unlike Impressionism, determining what is real is not a central issue.

As the central idea at the heart of Naturalism is Determinism, and the underlying issue of Impressionism is epistemology, so the dominant themes of Realism, beyond mimetic concerns, involve ethical crises. Moral choices are excluded from Naturalism by its deterministic emphasis, and to some extent from Impressionism by its problems in assessing what is real. Realism, on the other hand, assumes that a character knows what is real and that he is free to choose among alternatives presented to him, thus assuming full moral responsibility for his actions. As Åhnebrink suggests, the central decision made by Silas Lapham is representative of this theme, as are the decisions made by Marcia Gaylord in *A Modern Instance* and by Huck Finn in Twain's novel.

In Realism, the conflicts are often those moral and social dilemmas which grow out of bourgeois life and manners. As Jacob Kolb suggests, the ethics of *Huck Finn* are based upon the "confrontation of human beings in a humanely created social environment." As Realism subscribes to a normative common vision, it follows that the characters portrayed will also closely approximate the norm. As Kolb says,

> the realists write about the common, the average, the unextreme, the unrepresentative, the probable. They concern themselves with ordinary human lives seen in the context of normal social relationships. They concentrate on what people are rather than what ought to be, on men rather than Man.

One qualification that might be placed upon Kolb's description is that although Realistic characters are representative, they are also individualized, facing unique crises of intense moment drawn from within the range of probable human experience. They act as individuals, not as representatives or specimens. In this, characterization in Realism is not dramatically distinct from Impressionism, which emphasizes somewhat more the development of personality and ideas rather than their expression in moral judgment.

In narrative methodology, Realism demonstrates a great deal of variation. If nearly all Naturalism employs an omniscient narrator, and nearly all Impressionism some form of restrictive central intelligence, Realism tends toward Impressionism in its objectivity, eschewing omniscience and narrative intrusions. However, the effect of Realism is not generally to emphasize the limited knowledge of a character but to define his personality. First or third person limited, both usually identified with the mind of the protagonist, are the normative forms. This methodology allows for a natural definition of personality and for the documenting of the conflicts that give rise to the themes of Realism.

The structure of realistic fiction moves forward from character definition to ethical conflict, with the character's decision providing the climax and resolution of plot. Requiring neither the episodic units of Impressionism nor the loose and baggy ramblings of Naturalism, Realism can employ a great deal of structural variation. There is similar flexibility in the handling of figurative devices. Realism focuses on character and conflict; its frame of reference is personal rather than mythic and abstract. Realistic referential devices, therefore, grow out of context, and these are usually images and organic metaphors rather than symbols. For example, the houses in *The Rise of Silas Lapham* have a significance beyond themselves but one unique to Silas and his life, his social aspirations, his limitations. The same houses in other novels would have rather different values when related to characters of varying background. In short, the mimetic devices and themes of Realism relate to the basic concept of an ordinary character placed in a situation of ethical conflict. The fictional techniques, narrative methods, plot, and structural devices all derive from this underlying idea.

If these theoretical models of Realism, Naturalism, and Impressionism are artificial in their purity and imperfect as descriptions of individual works, they nevertheless postulate distinctions among the modes in theme and methodology. These lines of discrimination are crucial for an assessment of the works of Stephen Crane, who has been described variously as an innovative Impressionist, as the first American Naturalist, and as a central figure in the growth of Realism. Crane's work is sufficiently broad and varied so as to invite a variety of responses, but this variety deepens rather than vitiates the need to give his work a close reading in terms of discrete categories of literary modality. This is especially true for Impressionism, which has never received a full discussion in terms of Crane's work. His stories and novels need to be examined to determine which of them are essentially Impressionistic and what implications Impressionistic tendencies have for understanding the body of Crane's literary production. Crane, whom R. W. Stallman said "perfected more works than either Poe or Twain," played a key role in the development of American fiction, especially its transition from traditional thought and methods to what is now regarded as Modernism. A detailed examination of his fiction should help to define precisely what that role was and how it has influenced modern literature.

Chronology

1871   Born at Newark, New Jersey, November 1

1871–72   Crane family moves to Port Jervis, New York

1880   Father, Jonathan Townley Crane, dies

1882   Family relocates to Asbury Park, New Jersey; attends school there

1885   Writes first story, "Uncle Jake and the Bell Handle"; enrolls at Pennington Seminary, Pennington, New Jersey

1887   Withdraws from Pennington

1888   Enrolls at Hudson River Institute (Claverack College), Claverack, New York; works for brother, Townley Crane, at his press bureau at Asbury Park in the summer

1890   First sketch published, in school magazine *Vidette*; enters Lafayette College; fails classes and drops out at Christmas

1891   Transfers to Syracuse University; plays on varsity baseball team; works as correspondent for New York *Tribune*; first publication, "The King's Favor," appears in college magazine; writes early drafts of *Maggie*; quits school in June; meets Hamlin Garland in August; mother, Mary Helen Crane, dies in December

1892   Publishes five "Sullivan County Sketches" in New York *Tribune*; "Broken-Down Van" published; dismissed from *Tribune*

1893   Privately prints *Maggie: A Girl of the Streets* under pseudonym; begins writing *The Red Badge of Courage*

1894   Abridged version of *Red Badge of Courage* published in *Philadelphia Press*; other work published in *The Arena* and *New York Press*

1895   Writes articles for Bacheller-Johnson Syndicate in West and Mexico; *The Black Riders and Other Lines*; *Red Badge of Courage* published in full to enormous popularity, especially in England

1896   *George's Mother*; *The Little Regiment*; travels to Florida; meets Cora Taylor

1897   Wreck of *Commodore*; writes "The Open Boat"; covers Greco-Turkish War from April to May reporting for New York *Journal* and Westminster *Gazette*; Taylor accompanies him; Stephen and Cora settle in England; *The Third Violet*

1898   War correspondent during Spanish-American War for New York *World* and New York *Journal*; *The Open Boat and Other Tales of Adventure*; "The Bride Comes to Yellow Sky"; "Death and the Child"; "The Monster"; "The Blue Hotel"

1899   *War Is Kind*; *The Monster and Other Stories*; *Active Service*; debts accrue; returns to England to reside at Brede Manor; begins *The O'Ruddy*

1900   Dies of tuberculosis on June 5 in a sanitorium in Badenweiler, Germany; buried in Hillside, NJ. Posthumous publications: *Whilomville Stories*; *Wounds in the Rain*

Works by Stephen Crane

Sullivan County Sketches (1892)

Maggie: A Girl of the Streets (1893)

The Black Riders and Other Lines (1895), poems

The Red Badge of Courage: An Episode of the American Civil War (1895)

The Little Regiment and Other Episodes of the American Civil War (1896)

George's Mother (1896)

The Third Violet (1897)

The Open Boat and Other Tales of Adventure (1898)

War Is Kind (1899) poems

The Monster and Other Stories (1899)

Active Service (1899)

Wounds in the Rain: War Stories (1900)

Whilomville Stories (1900)

The O'Ruddy (1903)

Works about Stephen Crane

Adams, Henry. *The Education of Henry Adams.* 1918. Boston: Houghton Mifflin, 1961.

Bassan, Maurice, ed. *Stephen Crane's* Maggie: *Text and Context.* Belmont, Ca: Wadsworth, 1966.

Benfey, Christopher. *The Double Life of Stephen Crane.* New York: Alfred A. Knopf, 1992.

Bergon, Frank. *Stephen Crane's Artistry.* New York: College University Press, 1975.

Bloom, Harold, ed. *Stephen Crane.* New York: Chelsea House Press, 1987.

Bowers, Fredson, et. al., eds. *The University of Virginia Edition of Stephen Crane.* Charlottesville: University Press of Virginia, 1969.

Cady, Edwin H. *Stephen Crane.* Rev. ed. Boston: G.K. Hall-Twayne, 1980.

Colvert, James B. *Stephen Crane.* New York: Harcourt Brace Jovanovich, 1984.

Davis, Linda H. *Badge of Courage: The Life of Stephen Crane.* Boston: Houghton Mifflin, 1998.

Dooley, Patrick K. *The Pluralistic Philosophy of Stephen Crane.* Urbana: University of Illinois Press, 1993.

———. *Stephen Crane: An Annotated Bibliography of Secondary Scholarship.* New York: G. K. Hall, 1992.

Eye, Stephanie Bates. "Fact, Not Fiction: Questioning Our Assumptions about Crane's 'The Open Boat.'" *Studies in Short Fiction* 35.1 (1998 Winter): 65–76.

Brown, Bill. *The Material Unconscious: American Amusement, Stephen Crane, and the Economies of Play.* Cambridge: Harvard University Press, 1996.

Fried, Michael. *Realism, Writing, Disfiguration: On Thomas Eakins and Stephen Crane.* Chicago: University of Chicago Press, 1987.

Gibson, Donald B. *The Fiction of Stephen Crane.* Carbondale, Illl.: Southern Illinois University Press, 1968.

———, ed. The Red Badge of Courage*: Redefining the Hero.* Boston: Twayne-G. K. Hall, 1988.

Green, Carol Hurd. "Stephen Crane and the Fallen Woman." *American Novelists Revisited: Essays in Feminist Criticism.* Ed. Fritz Fleischman. Boston: G. K. Hall, 1982.

Halliburton, David. *The Color of the Sky: A Study of Stephen Crane.* Cambridge: Cambridge University Press, 1989.

Hoffman, Daniel. *The Poetry of Stephen Crane.* New York: Columbia University Press, 1957.

Holton, Milne. *Cylinder of Vision: The Fiction and Journalistic Writing of Stephen Crane.* Baton Rouge: Louisiana State University Press, 1972.

Horwitz, Howard. "*Maggie* and the Sociological Paradigm." *American Literary History* 10.4 (1998 Winter): 606–38.

Kelly, Richard J. and Alan K. Lathrop, eds. *Recovering Crane: Essays on a Poet.* Ann Arbor: University of Michigan Press, 1993.

Knapp, Bettina L. *Stephen Crane.* New York: Ungar, 1987.

LaFrance, Marston. "Private Fleming: His Various Battles." *A Reading of Stephen Crane.* Oxford UK: Oxford-Clarendon, 1971.

Linson, Corwin K. *My Stephen Crane.* Ed. Edwin H. Cady. Syracuse: Syracuse University Press, 1958.

Mitchell, Lee Clark. *New Essays on* The Red Badge of Courage. Cambridge: Cambridge University Press, 1986.

Monteiro, George. *Stephen Crane's Blue Badge of Courage.* Baton Rouge: Louisiana State University Press, 2000.

Nagel, James. *Stephen Crane and Literary Impressionism.* University Park: The Pennsylvania State University Press, 1980.

Pizer, Donald. "*The Red Badge of Courage*: Text, Theme, and Form." *South Atlantic Quarterly* 84 (1985 Spring): 313–330.

———, ed. *Critical Essays on Stephen Crane's* The Red Badge of Courage. Boston: G.K. Hall, 1990.

Rich, Charlotte. "Nora Black and the New Woman in Active Service." *War, Literature, and the Arts: An International Journal of the Humanities* (1999): 23–35.

Seltzer, Mark. "Statistical Persons." *Bodies and Machines*. New York: Routledge, 1992.

Solomon, Eric. *Stephen Crane in England*. Cambridge: Harvard University Press, 1964.

Stallman, Robert W. *Stephen Crane: A Biography*. New York: George Braziller, 1968.

———. "Stephen Crane: A Revaluation." *Critical Essays on Stephen Crane's* The Red Badge of Courage. Ed. Donald Pizer. Boston: G.K. Hall, 1990.

Sufrin, Mark. *Stephen Crane*. New York: Atheneum, 1992.

Walcutt, Charles C. "Stephen Crane: Naturalist." *Critical Essays on Stephen Crane's* The Red Badge of Courage. Ed. Donald Pizer. Boston: G. K. Hall, 1990.

Weatherford, Richard M., ed. *Stephen Crane: The Critical Heritage*. London: Routledge-Kegan Paul, 1973.

Wertheim, Stanley. "Introduction." *The Correspondence of Stephen Crane*. 2 Vol. New York: Columbia University Press, 1988.

Wertheim, Stanley and Paul Sorrentino. *The Crane Log: A Documentary Life of Stephen Crane, 1871–1900*. Boston: G. K. Hall, 1993.

———, "Thomas Beer: The Clay Feet of Stephen Crane Biography." *American Literary Realism* 22.3 (1990 Spring): 2–16.

Wertheim, Stanley and Paul Sorrentino, eds. *The Correspondence of Stephen Crane*. New York: Columbia University Press, 1988.

Wolford, Chester L. *Stephen Crane: A Study of the Short Fiction*. Boston: Twayne Publishers, 1989.

WEBSITES

The Stephen Crane Society
www.gonzaga.edu/faculty/campbell/crane

DMS Stephen Crane Page
http://www3.uakron.edu/english/richards/edwards/crane.html

About Stephen Crane
http://www.underthesun.cc/Classics/Crane/

Paul Sorrentino: In Search of the "Real" Stephen Crane: Excerpts from the Opening Plenary Session, 2000 National CEA Conference
http://www.as.ysu.edu/~english/cea/sorrentino.html

American Poems: Stephen Crane
www.americanpoems.com/poets/stephencrane/

Red Badge Home Page
http://xroads.virginia.edu/~HYPER/CRANE/title.html

Stephen Crane's "The Open Boat"
An interactive hypertext study guide that invites commentary and annotation from visitors.
http://sites.unc.edu/storyforms/openboat/

Contributors

HAROLD BLOOM is Sterling Professor of the Humanities at Yale University and Henry W. and Albert A. Berg Professor of English at the New York University Graduate School. He is the author of over 20 books, including *Shelly's Mythmaking* (1959), *The Visionary Company* (1961), *Blake's Apocalypse* (1963), *Yeats* (1970), *A Map of Misreading* (1975), *Kabbalah and Criticism* (1975), *Agon: Toward a Theory of Revisionism* (1982), *The American Religion* (1992), *The Western Canon* (1994), and *Omens of Millennium: The Gnosis of Angels, Dreams, and Resurrection* (1996). *The Anxiety of Influence* (1973) sets forth Professor Bloom's provocative theory of the literary relationships between the great writers and their predecessors. His most recent books include *Shakespeare: The Invention of the Human*, a 1998 National Book Award finalist, and *How to Read and Why*, which was published in 2000. In 1999, Professor Bloom received the prestigious American Academy of Arts and Letters Gold Medal for Criticism.

NORMA JEAN LUTZ is a freelance writer who lives in Tulsa, Oklahoma. She is the author of more than 250 short stories and articles as well as over 50 books of fiction and nonfiction.

ROBERT GUNN is a doctoral candidate in the Department of English and American Literature at New York University, where he is writing a dissertation on the ethics of historical representation and the American Romance.

ROBERT WOOSTER STALLMAN was among the foremost scholars of Stephen Crane throughout his distinguished career. In addition to his omnibus edition of Crane's writings and scholarly biography of Crane, Stallman also published critical work on Henry James, Joseph Conrad, Thornton Wilder, and F. Scott Fitzgerald.

JAMES NAGEL is the J. O. Eidson Distinguished Professor of American Literature at the University of Georgia, Athens. Professor Nagel is the founder of the distinguished scholarly journal *Studies in American Fiction*. His books include *Ernest Hemingway: The Writer in Context*; *The Portable American Realism Reader*; and *Hemingway in Love and War*. He is currently at work on a study of American Impressionism from 1890 to 1930.

Index